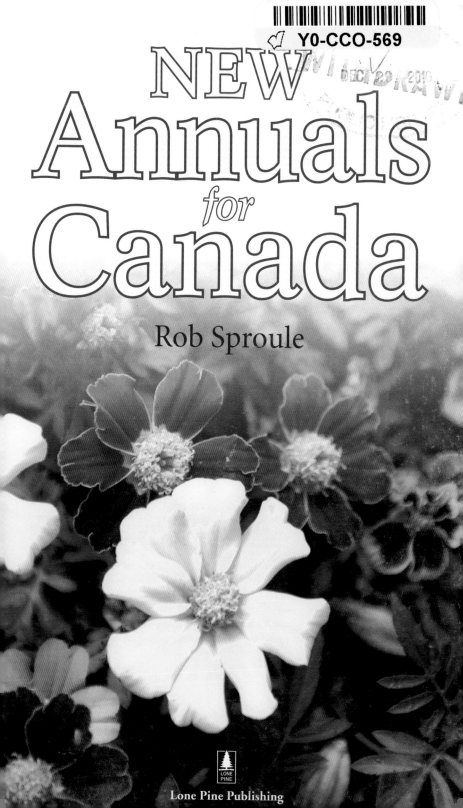

# NEW
# Annuals *for*
# Canada

## Rob Sproule

Lone Pine Publishing

**Lone Pine Publishing**
10145 – 81 Avenue
Edmonton, Alberta T6E 1W9

Website: www.lonepinepublishing.com

**Library and Archives Canada Cataloguing in Publication**

Sproule, Rob, 1978-
          New annuals for Canada / Rob Sproule.

Includes index.
ISBN 978-1-55105-841-2

          1. Annuals (Plants)--Canada. 2. Gardening--Canada. I. Title.

SB422.S685 2010          635.9'3120971          C2009-905881-2

*Editorial Director:* Nancy Foulds
*Project Editor:* Sheila Quinlan
*Production Manager:* Gene Longson
*Book Design and Layout:* Rob Tao
*Cover Design:* Gerry Dotto

*Photo Credits:* All photos are by Rob Sproule, except: Ball Horticultural 41b, 63b, 67a, 74, 80, 81, 85b, 167, 175b, 223a, 227b; Cunningham Photo 10; Tamara Eder 37a, 38, 39a; Lyndsey Hahn 19; Tim Matheson 37b; Curtis Morie 29, 32, 34; Megan Mundell 13a, 15, 18, 22, 36, 52, 67b, 83b, 105b, 109b, 113, 137, 148, 154, 182, 203a, 205a, 207a&b, 217b, 221a&b, 225, 229b, 240; Proven Winners 16, 40, 42, 43b, 47, 49b, 53a&b, 56, 57a&b, 58b, 59a, 61b, 64, 65a, 66, 69b, 78a, 79b, 90, 92, 94, 98, 99b, 106, 120, 121a&b, 122, 123b, 130, 136, 138, 142, 143, 146, 147a&b, 150, 151a&b, 152, 156, 157b, 158, 160, 162, 163a, 185a&b, 189a, 190, 194, 196, 204, 206, 210, 220, 222, 223b, 231a&b, 232, 235; Robert Ritchie 39b; Sandy Weatherall 1, 72, 73a, 88a, 89b, 131, 132b, 176, 178b, 230.

We acknowledge the financial support of the Government of Canada through the Book Publishing Industry Development Program (BPIDP) for our publishing activities.

PC: *PC15*

# Contents

# Dedication

To Meg, the source of all my joy.

# Acknowledgements

First and foremost, thanks to Meg, my mom, dad and entire family for always believing in me. I couldn't have asked for a more supportive family. Thanks also to the entire staff at Salisbury Greenhouse, who helped make this book possible with their many insights and ideas; it's a pleasure to work with you all. Thanks to my co-owners for giving me the time I needed to write a book I could be proud of. Thank you to Lone Pine for taking a chance on a new author. To those who helped me with this book, whether it was a suggestion or hands-on help, including my fellow partners, thank you. Big thanks to the many people and companies who opened their yards, grounds and businesses to me and my camera, including Salisbury Greenhouse, Proven Winners, Meg Mundell, Val MacMillan, Cindy Mundell, Luella Chmelyk, JVK, Ball Horticultural Company, Wellington Garden Centre, Muttart Conservatory and Earls Restaurants. Thank you to Meg for being my partner in photography and for taking some of the best shots.

# The Plants at a Glance

Pictorial Guide in Alphabetical Order

**Abutilon**
p. 40

**Ageratum**
p. 42

**Alstroemeria**
p. 44

**Begonia—Tuberous**
p. 46

**Black-Eyed Susan**
p. 50

**Cobbity Daisy**
p. 52

**Crown of Thorns**
p. 54

**Dahlia**
p. 56

**Dianthus**
p. 60

**Diascia**
p. 62

**Euphorbia**
p. 64

**Gazania**
p. 66

**Heliotrope**
p. 68

**Impatiens—Double**
p. 70

Impatiens—New Guinea
p. 72

Laurentia
p. 74

Osteospermum
p. 76

Pansy
p. 80

Pentas
p. 84

Petunia—Upright
p. 86

Schizanthus
p. 90

Strawflower
p. 92

Alternanthera
p. 94

Baby Tears
p. 96

Begonia—Rex
p. 98

Coleus
p. 100

Croton
p. 104

Eucalyptus
p. 106

Ferns
p. 108

Herbs
p. 112

Iresine
p. 116

Kale
p. 118

Oxalis
p. 120

Strobilanthes
p. 122

Succulents
p. 124

Talinum
p. 128

Bacopa
p. 130

Begonia—Trailing
p. 134

Bidens
p. 136

Flambe
p. 138

Fuchsia
p. 140

Lantana
p. 142

Lobularia
p. 144

Million Bells
p. 146

Nemesia
p. 150

Petunia—Trailing
p. 152

Phlox
p. 156

Scaevola
p. 158

Torenia
p. 160

Verbena—Trailing
p. 162

Agrostis
p. 164

Black-Eyed Susan Vine
p. 166

Bougainvillea
p. 168

Cobaea
p. 170

Creeping Jenny
p. 172

Dichondra
p. 174

Mandevilla
p. 176

Passion Vine
p. 180

Sweet Pea
p. 182

Sweet Potato Vine
p. 184

Tropical Vines
p. 186

Alocasia and Colocasia
p. 190

Angelonia
p. 194

Banana
p. 196

Bromeliads
p. 198

Brugmansia and Datura
p. 202

Canna Lily
p. 204

Cleome
p. 206

Cosmos—Chocolate
p. 208

Gaura
p. 210

Hibiscus
p. 212

Peppers
p. 214

Sunflower
p. 216

Trachelium
p. 218

Cordyline
p. 220

Juncus
p. 222

Millet
p. 224

Phormium
p. 226

Purple Fountain Grass
p. 228

Sedge
p. 230

Stipa
p. 232

# Foreword

Creativity is the heart of gardening. When we garden, whether we're designing, planting or nurturing plants into bloom, we're creating. In the modern world, it's rare that we have the ability to create with our own hands; gardening gives us that chance. It's one of the most beloved and widespread passions in the world, and, like all passions that survive the passage of time, it is constantly evolving and adapting to stay relevant.

I've lived in the world of gardening my whole life, and over the last 15 years I've watched both how rapidly it has changed and how ardently it has remained the same. I grew up working in my father's greenhouse, which he inherited from his father, and many of the major life lessons that I carry with me I learned from watching and thinking about plants.

Through thousands of conversations with gardeners about everything from colour schemes to nibbly rabbits, I've begun to understand that gardeners have a connection with plants that runs much deeper than growing pretty flowers.

Salisbury Greenhouse was founded by Helen and Fred Sproule in 1965, and we've grown to be one of the largest and most trusted garden centres in Alberta. The heart and soul of our business is in growing. In over four covered acres of greenhouse we grow millions of plants year-round (and if I may say so, we've become exceedingly good at it). Recently, my two brothers and I, along with my father, became the third generation of family owners at Salisbury. Adam, the oldest, operates a landscaping division of the company while Dave and I work in the front lines of the evolving gardening industry.

Helen and Fred Sproule founded Salisbury in 1965.

We're young owners, each in our 30s, and we see the world of gardening through enthusiastic eyes. I'm 32 and was married four years ago to the love of my life. Three years ago we moved into a suburban house with a big lot on a street that is full of new families like ours. Each lot has a mature yard that has already had decades of love poured into it, just waiting to be rediscovered and redefined by the next generation of gardeners.

My formal schooling is in English literature; I'm wrapping up a Master of Arts degree with a thesis of autobiographical poetry about mountaineering in the Canadian Rockies. That I have devoted my career to plants may seem like an odd fit—the academic life is often a long way from gardening—but it's actually a perfect fit. Humans have adored plants since before we could write on walls, and our history is inseparable from their history. I am also fascinated with plants themselves, and I find a blooming passion flower or a sprouting bean seed as interesting and complex as any philosophy book. I marvel that their engineering and beauty always manages to slightly evade articulation. I love watching people react to plants, and when they come through the greenhouse's front door with a face gaunt after a stressful day and find themselves lingering, sometimes for hours, spontaneously exploring the complexities and delicacies of plant life, it reminds me that our desire to grow and nurture and harvest is not an invented want but an ancient need. As a strange blend of poet and businessman, I consider plants to be as much my muse as they are my livelihood.

It's a privilege to share my life with plants and to spend time watching them grow, and it's a privilege to be able to share some of my enthusiasm with you in this book. I hope you learn from it and are inspired by it. I believe that gardening books need to do more than tell you about light levels and growth habits; they should inspire you to be creative and try new plants and techniques and to discover—or rediscover—the unchanging and simple joy of getting your hands dirty and watching the plants you've nourished grow, bloom and nourish you in return.

The joy of watching something grow is part of gardening that never changes, no matter what the trends are doing.

# Introduction

Gardening has endured for millennia because it's both endlessly versatile and refreshingly constant. Some aspects of it evolve and adapt, and other aspects never change. Wherever there is a seed and some dirt, we can garden. Our need to make things grow and our essential love of flowers never changes, nor does the joy we feel when we first get dirt under our fingernails after a long winter, as if we are reconnecting with a dear friend. What is constantly evolving in gardening is how we grow and think about the plants themselves and what we can do with them. In this book I will do my best to articulate the change that I've witnessed from the frontlines of the gardening world.

Over many years in this industry, I've charted the evolution of how gardeners are thinking about annuals. It used to be that people were most interested in "the basics"— where a plant came from and how to grow it and take care of it. That's still important, but gardeners are becoming more interested in learning about the plant in the broader context of the colour and style of their yard. Most of the annuals we sell now are destined for some kind of container, and in many yards containers provide the bulk of the colour, meaning that new varieties of annuals are increasingly bred specifically to coordinate with others. Annual gardening is becoming more like fashion; it's about accessorizing the yard and making it, in the words of many a flamboyant fashion designer, "fabulous!"

With every annual in this book I have three goals and, if I accomplish them with a few plants while you're reading, I'll consider the book successful. My goals are:

- to make you fall in love with the plants
- to make you confident that you can take care of them
- to inspire you to be creative with them.

Gardening is about creativity, and if I've done my job this book will give you some of the inspiration and the practical know-how necessary to try something new. Nothing about gardening should be a chore. To me, it's a privilege to be able to get my hands in the soil, even if it's to do a mundane task. I'm passionate about plants because I think that gardening is the most life-affirming thing a person can do, and I hope that this book makes you a little more passionate, too.

## Changing Trends in Gardening

Gardening is the most popular and fastest-growing hobby in North America, and more people than ever before are making growing a valued part of their lives. We're intoxicated by the sight of a crocus pushing itself up through the snow, or of thick yellow bushels of black-eyed Susans in September, and it's no surprise to me why. Plants ask for almost nothing and give everything back, pouring

Two examples of just how creative you can get! On the left is a living container made with sedums and herbs from Quebec City, and on the right is a whimsical "Flower Margarita" that you can easily make with cut flowers from the garden.

oxygen into our environment and spontaneously splashing colours across our yards and lives like a mad painter. After a day amid the sharp angles and halogen lights of offices, people naturally begin to crave the soft fragrances and rich air of their yards for a sense of peace and regeneration. Gardening is the most life-affirming hobby in the world because it's the only hobby that takes care of you as much as you take care of it.

Gardening is much more than a hobby, however. It's a cultural phenomenon. Its rich history stretches back thousands of years and is as complex as the history of any nation. Anyone who wasn't a nobleman caught growing a chrysanthemum in ancient China was beheaded. In the Middle Ages, monks carefully tended their walled gardens as a way of becoming closer to God. In 17th- and 18th-century France, the very rich showcased their wealth by constructing massive, perfectly ordered gardens, such as the one at the palace of Versailles. These symbols of opulence fuelled the flames of the bloody revolution that ultimately led to democracy. Columbus sailed not for gold but for spices, and many early explorers risked their lives to wade into unknown forests and jungles in search of new plants for the gardeners back home in England, France and Spain to experiment with. Most of the annuals we enjoy every year came from these expeditions. How we garden, where we garden and what we put into our gardens is always changing to reflect

our culture, but the thing that has always remained the same is why we garden. We garden, like the Middle Ages monks and the Empress Josephine gardened, to nourish ourselves.

The last 10 years have seen a huge shift in how we garden in Canada, a shift that's been one of the most dramatic and rapid in history. Before I discuss that shift, however, allow me to put it in context with a very brief summary of 20th-century gardening.

In most parts of Canada, gardening didn't become popular until after World War II, when there was a massive housing boom to accommodate returning soldiers and their new families. The single-family home began to appear in great numbers, heralding the first golden age of suburbia and of gardening. In the suburbs, each family had a yard of its own, and the prosperity of the 1950s allowed people more time to spend in their yard. Gardening was suddenly the fastest-growing hobby in Canada, and garden centres began popping up everywhere to meet the demand. Usually they were little more than a cold-frame or two that opened for a couple of months in spring and then closed for winter.

Until the early 1990s, the front yard of an average suburban house often looked very much like the neighbour's front yard. There would be one or two large flower beds in the yard. In the centre of each was a shrub, often a potentilla or an evergreen (which may have come home from school with a child on Arbour Day). There might be a few perennials around the shrub, depending on the size of the bed. The perennials tended to be the most expendable part of the front yard garden. The essential part of the garden were the bedding plants that rimmed the edge and were as bright and vibrant as possible. Standard fare was to put red geraniums at the back, with a crisp line of yellow marigolds in the centre and white alyssum for a border. Those bold enough to plant in a container often did so with a dracaena spike in the centre, with red geraniums and some petunias or marigolds around. The only reliable trailing plant available was lobelia, and it was found in almost every container.

Flower beds like these used to be where almost all "bedding plants" were planted; that has changed.

In garden centres, annuals were sold in six-packs—plastic containers with six cells that held six small plants that were very rarely large enough to bloom. The customer bought the six-pack, planted the contents on the May long weekend, and waited. June was the waiting month, time allocated for the plants to grow large enough to bloom. The bedding plants of the day often grew at a frustratingly slow pace, and it often wasn't until the middle to end of July that they finally erupted into full bloom and the yard was alive and beautiful. August was spent enjoying the colour and trying not to think about the dreaded first frosts, which sometimes came as early as mid-September. As short as the bedding plant season was, gardeners persisted, year after year, in putting hours of labour into making their yards, if even for a short time, a celebration of colour. To me, the popularity of gardening in the 1970s, 80s and early 90s, despite the frustratingly short season and the amount of work it required, is a testament to the power of colour and of our desire to create something beautiful that we can call our own.

In the early 1990s, a company called Proven Winners introduced a plant called bacopa. Initially, bacopa was a stringy, nondescript and rather pungent little plant that many greenhouse growers dismissed outright. Gardeners, however, had other ideas and bought up bacopa as soon as it hit the shelves, with an enthusiasm that made growers and producers sit up and take notice. The container gardening craze had begun!

Bacopa: this little white flower changed the way we think about gardening.

Bacopa's popularity was the result of it being a high performance annual, and instead of being sold in a six-pack, it was sold in a pot (usually with a 10 cm diameter) so that gardeners didn't have to spend half the season waiting for it to mature. Not long after bacopa was introduced, a company called Ball unveiled the Wave petunia. The Wave was an even bigger success than bacopa and quickly became the most popular annual in history! Waves were even faster growing than bacopa, trailing 90 cm in a single season (even a prairie season), a feat unheard of at the time. Whiskey barrels, clay pots, window boxes and even wheelbarrows overflowing with Waves quickly became as common a sight as pots full of geraniums. New varieties of high performance annuals were introduced every year, and before long plants such as million bells, verbena and diascia occupied the same prime benches in garden centres as marigolds and geraniums did only a few years before.

Around the same time as the introduction of high performance annuals, people increasingly began to spend more energy and money on gardening in the backyard rather than the front. Throughout the mid and late 1990s, the front flower beds that once lined suburban streets with geranium red and alyssum white slowly filled with the more economical, less-hassle perennials, and backyards, hidden from view, filled with life. This shift happened, in my opinion, for two reasons. The first is economical.

High performance annuals are much more expensive than six-packs, and they made mass plantings in big front yard beds costly operations. The second reason is much more personal. I believe that the turbulence and uncertainty of world events in the last decade, especially since 2001, have inspired people to think less about maintaining outward appearances and to think more about spending time with their families and the people they love. Gardeners began to make their backyard decks, patios and gazebos more comfortable and inviting by decorating them with carefully planted and well-loved containers. Sales of yard furniture, yard lighting, mosquito repellents and anything having to do with spending more time outside ("outdoor living" being the buzz word) have increased dramatically since 2001. Canadians are investing their gardening dollars into spending summer evenings with the people they love in the privacy of their backyards.

Gardening has also become much more popular in cities, where apartment balconies boast more containers than ever before. Container gardening is all about gardening in small spaces, and the amount of choices suddenly available has made gardening not only possible but also exciting to many apartment and condo dwellers.

Garden centres have also changed considerably. With high performance annuals came a new emphasis on the

Canadian garden centres have begun to pay more attention to international gardening trends and styles.

gardening consumer. Aisles, once notoriously narrow, became wide enough for a woman to push a baby carriage through or couples to walk through hand in hand. Concrete was poured and tile was laid down so that people didn't have to walk in the mud anymore, and many garden centres installed coffee bars and even sandwich bars. Gardening, once considered a rural or suburban pastime, was reaching out to a whole new audience.

At our garden centre, we spend a lot of time thinking about how to attract the next generation of gardeners. Although I rarely meet someone who doesn't enjoy gardening, many young people don't feel that they have the practical know-how to do it well, and without the know-how backing you up it's very hard to be creative (which always involves taking a chance). While the May garden shopping day is often a significant rite of spring for many Baby Boomers, eagerly planning their garden as they dip out of one garden centre and into another, many people in my generation feel overwhelmed when they walk into a large garden centre, so they often buy their plants at the box store with the rest of their groceries. One of my most important jobs at Salisbury in the last few years has been to reach out to my peers, to 30-somethings with young families and no green-thumb in sight, and show them how fun and easy gardening can be. The young families who are moving into their first homes across Canada, whether it's a suburban bungalow or an urban apartment with a balcony, will be the ones who will define how we garden over the next decades. Hopefully some of you are reading this book, possibly because you feel drawn toward gardening but don't know where to start. I hope this helps you become acquainted enough with the basic know-how to be comfortable being creative, and inspired enough thinking about what you can create to want to try something new.

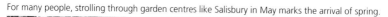

For many people, strolling through garden centres like Salisbury in May marks the arrival of spring.

## The Layout of this Book

Probably most of the annuals people buy today are destined to be planted in some kind of container garden. That's why it's impossible to write a gardening book about annuals, especially new annuals, without spending a lot of time talking about how to use them in containers. Unlike trees, shrubs or even perennials, annuals are often defined by the other annuals around them, just as a song lyric makes most sense when you hear the whole verse. I've given this book a unique layout to reflect the changing way that annuals are being used. Instead of being organized alphabetically A to Z, I've divided the annuals into categories that reflect the basic elements of a container.

The three elements of a container are often referred to as thrillers, fillers and spillers. I'm not very fond of this phrasing, but it gets the point across. A thriller is the tallest element, usually in the centre or the back of the container. I have two categories for this element in the book: "Centrepieces" and "Grasses." The filler in a container is the plant (or plants) that fills it out and usually gives it the bulk of its colour. My two categories in the book for this element are "Upright Colour," which covers the fillers that flower, and "Foliage," which covers the fillers that either don't bloom or aren't known for their blooms and are used to provide a contrasting splash of leaves and texture to the mix. You'll find the spillers, or the trailing plants, in the sections "Trailing Colour," which contains trailing plants known for their flowers, and "Vines," which are trailing plants better known for their foliage. It's not a perfect system. For example, some vines prefer to grow upward on a trellis, making them better fit as a centrepiece, but for the most part the plants are in the right places. If you're planning on putting a container together, my hope is that these categories will help you in the design process.

This book's title is *New Annuals for Canada*, but you'll quickly notice that many of the plants in here have been known to Canadian gardeners for some time. "New annuals" doesn't refer just to the plants themselves but to the new and creative ways we're using plants in our gardens. For many of the entries in the book, the "new" is in the creative ways in which gardeners are rediscovering old classics, whether it's houseplants being worked into container gardens or herbs being used as ornamentals.

Along with growth habit, colour is an essential part of any container. Many people use a colour wheel like this one.

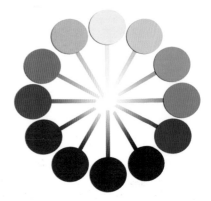

As for the contents of the book, I've made a point of only including annuals that are readily available. It's frustrating to all parties when someone falls in love with a plant that is almost impossible to find. You'll have to call around for some of the plants in this book, but if you're close to a large population centre you should be able to find everything.

As a grower I'm sceptical about the performance of an annual until I can see it with my own eyes. Garden performance (how will it look three months after I've planted it) is the most important issue in gardening. I've seen every variety in the book (except for a few new ones that I make note of) grow and perform before recommending it. Annuals are big business to some very big companies, and there's a ton of marketing out there trying to tell you who has the best plants. My job is to look past all the marketing and judge their garden performance, and in this book only the best performers are recommended.

Look past the hype; the plant is what is important.

## The Top Five Questions

Garden centres are the front lines of the rapidly changing world of gardening, where beginners and experts alike come to browse, mingle and chat about their ideas and inspirations. It's through my daily conversations with gardeners that I learn which plants, colours and trends have the most buzz and which ones are "so last season." All those conversations and questions have also taught me that the majority of the questions about plants, from "what can I put in a hot, dry location" to "will these two plants go well together," can be summed up in the five categories that follow. My hope is that I can answer these questions for you right off the bat for each plant so that you can move on to the really important part of getting excited about planting it. The symbols will also make it easy to see what plants are good container-mates with others when you're in the garden centre choosing your plants.

Most Asked Question #1: Size and Habit

Every account will tell you how high and wide your annual will eventually get. Of course, the final size will vary with region. Annuals in regions that receive cold nights into June may not grow to the same size as they would in warmer regions. You'll notice with many annuals that the size depends on the variety and can often range dramatically; for these plants I've included the sizes with each variety. When choosing your annuals, it's also important to think about their shape, especially if you're choosing annuals to plant together in a container. There are usually three central elements in a container:

Try to keep the size of the plants and the pots in a balanced proportion—unless you have giant pots like these that you want to show off.

*Centrepiece plants* provide the vertical focal point and are often the most striking architectural feature. Their shape ranges from very vertical (millet, cleome) to more loosely vertical and airy (guara, purple fountain grass) to lush, leafy and just plain large (canna lily, hibiscus). The shape of your centrepiece plant will usually determine the shape of your container garden, so it's important to look at the habit of the plant in addition to the numeric height and spread.

*Central plants (fillers)*, either flowering or foliage, will provide the body and the bulk of your container. They typically have a mounding habit. When you're choosing them, keep in mind the proportion of their size to the size of the rest of the elements in your container.

*Trailing plants* are cascading plants that flow out of the container. They provide a sense of height to the container garden and soften the container itself. Some trailing plants have more volume than others and may compete with your filler plants for space. For example, million bells are usually called trailers, but they are also robust filler plants, so you might want to leave some room for them to grow upward as well as down. Conversely, bacopa will tend to trail right away.

Keeping shape and habit, as well as height and spread, in mind while you're choosing annuals will help you choose plants that fit neatly into your vision.

Most Asked Question #2: Exposure
Plants can't go and find shade if it's too hot for them. They are stuck where we plant them, and because for most annuals our garden is a long, long way from their original homeland, we have to approximate where they want to be. I think of a garden centre as a United Nations of plants. The annuals you browse through in spring have been pulled from the four corners of the earth, and a plant native to the deep jungles of Colombia might be on the bench beside one from the Namibian desert (and the journey from there to the garden centre is usually fascinating). An annual will thrive most if it's planted in a spot that mimics the conditions of the area where it has evolved and grown for thousands of years; that's why with each annual

Cacti are an excellent choice for the hottest, driest areas.

I endeavour to tell you where the plant is native to. If you have a fiery south exposure then it's helpful to know which plant came from the open Australian scrubland, or if your yard is sunny but the light is dappled under trees, then you might want to choose European woodland plants that will appreciate it most.

I will often make caveats in the book for different exposure levels in different parts of the country. Canada is a massive country with many climatic regions. The most important factor for our purposes is the intensity of the sunlight. Although more humid areas of the country, namely those near the coast and as far inland as southern Ontario in the east and central BC in the west, can get very hot, the high humidity tempers the sun's intensity so that plants can handle more exposure. Annuals that love humidity, such as begonias and impatiens, love these humid areas. The geographic centre of Canada, namely the prairies and NWT, are cooler but drier, so the sun is very intense. Some plants that thrive in full sun in humid regions will potentially wilt or burn in full sun on the prairies. I will warn you if full exposure plants are not suitable for dry heat.

Each plant description comes with one of three symbols.

means that the plant needs at least six hours of good sunlight to perform at its best. Less sunlight will probably start to cause its original compact, pleasing habit to get leggy quickly and its foliage to turn a paler shade of green. Many full-sun plants are also drought-tolerant plants that have adapted to arid conditions. These plants are ideal for your south-facing deck or patio, under the white siding that reflects the sun.

 indicates a plant that still needs a good amount of sun but will need to be protected from the afternoon sun. Exposure to morning sun is perfect for these plants, but they will typically also do well in dappled afternoon sun (e.g., south exposure but sheltered by large trees) or evening sun.

indicates annuals that need to be sheltered. These plants often come from tropical regions where very little sunlight filters down to the jungle floor. They are typically good for areas that receive partial sun, but they can tolerate less. All annuals love sun; it's the intensity of the sun that they need to be sheltered from. In Miami, New Guinea impatiens grow in full southern exposures, but the humidity there is extremely high. Ultimately, it's trial and error to see what will grow best in the different areas of your yard.

Most Asked Question #3: Moisture
The amount of water a plant gets is arguably the most important factor of its development. As with sunlight, the amount of water a plant needs is largely a product of its native land.

Root systems evolve in response to the amount of water that is available in their environment, and if a plant gets a dramatically different amount of water than what it needs or is accustomed to over a sustained period of time, the roots won't be able to properly deal with it and the plant will suffer.

Because a container is a closed space, there's less room for error than there is in the ground; containers dry out faster. If you're a person who doesn't have much time to spend in the garden and needs containers that are low maintenance, then you won't want to pack high moisture plants tightly together into a small pot, or you'll have to water them all the time. Watering is a time-consuming aspect of gardening, and while some people find it to be a relaxing end to a day at the office, others see it as a chore and, though they may love their garden, want to do as little of it as possible. If you plant high moisture or high performance plants (such as trailing petunias), you will need to water them more often. However, these are often the plants that really put the "wow" factor into your garden, providing the lush tropical leaves and the avalanches of flowers that provide the finishing touches.

The droplet symbol is designed to tell you how much water your plant needs to perform at its best. Telling you the amount of water a plant needs isn't just for its well-being, but for yours as well. Most of the annuals we sell at the greenhouse are destined to be planted in containers, usually with other annuals. If you're a gardener who wants to incorporate many different types of plants into the garden, then you'll want to match container-mates that have similar moisture requirements. For example, if you plant bacopa (high moisture) with

Giant hanging baskets like this Supertunia are showstoppers, but unless you transplant them they will need a lot of water during hot weather.

Pro-Mix is an excellent peat based medium that allows roots to grow quickly, but you'll need to water your plant a bit more often as well.

drying up. Always water until the water flows from the bottom of the container to make sure all the soil is moistened. If you've let it get bone dry, you may have to water it twice. If you have a saucer under the plant, make sure to empty it of run-off or rain water. Arid-loving plants universally hate wet feet, and their roots rot easily. These plants are good to get if you're going to be away for much of the summer.

succulents (low moisture), it will be very hard to keep both of them healthy.

means that the plant is drought tolerant and more likely to appreciate sandy, very well-drained soil. These plants have often evolved in arid regions and often have small, fragile root systems because they have come to rely on small amounts of surface water. Keep this feature in mind when you're transplanting them into your garden. Drought-tolerant plants don't like to be plunked into large containers; often the pot you buy them in will suffice for the season. If you do transplant one into a large container, make sure the soil medium drains freely. Allow the surface of the soil to dry visibly between waterings, but remember that it's not healthy for any plant to wilt. If you plant in a peat moss based mix, water it when the medium pulls slightly away from the sides of the container, which indicates that the spongy peat fibres are

indicates the plants like their moisture level just right. I still recommend a freely draining medium and an empty saucer (or no saucer at all) underneath. When the surface begins to dry, put your finger in the soil to test the moisture. If your finger is dry to the first knuckle, it's time to water.

means the plants are often tropical or marginal and need to be kept consistently moist. When the surface of the soil is beginning to dry out, water it. If you want to take an extra step to ensure the health of your plants, put a layer of cedar mulch on the soil in your container. Mulch isn't just for perennial and shrub beds; in a container it prevents evaporation and looks and smells wonderful.

Just because a plant needs a lot of water doesn't mean that it can be planted in muddy soil that doesn't drain very well, or in a pot with no holes. Lots of water doesn't mean stagnant water. Plant roots pull oxygen out of the water just like fish gills and will deoxygenate stagnant water until the plant drowns in it. At the garden centre we plant all of our plants, whether they need little or lots of moisture, in the same very well-drained medium; the difference is in the amount we water.

Most Asked Question #4: Fertilizer
Fertilizers are big business, and as such gardeners are inundated with commercials, hype and hyperbole about the latest holy water that you just can't do without. Most of the annuals being introduced every year (especially those with the most publicity) are very high feeders. They are like race cars that need high octane fuel; they have been bred to grow in an unsustainable sprint, exhausting themselves by the end of the season, and they need lots of supplements to do it. So when we are talking about new annuals, we're inevitably talking about fertilizing. There are two groups of fertilizers—organic and inorganic—and each group has its advantages and disadvantages. Before you believe the next commercial you see, let's cut through the hype and get down to the basics.

*Inorganic fertilizers:* these are the N-P-K fertilizers, most commonly the water solubles that turn your water a light blue. In the short term, inorganics are the most potent fertilizers, but they are also becoming increasingly controversial, as we'll see below. There are many brands, but they are all combinations of three basic elements: nitrogen (N), phosphorus (P) and potassium (K).

The numbers represent the percentage of the element in the fertilizer; the higher the number, the more punch that particular element is packing. The numbers rarely add up to 100 percent; the rest is filler.

The next question is, "What do the different combinations do?" The answer is, "Top, down, all-around." Nitrogen (top) promotes healthy foliage and leaf growth. If your plant isn't getting enough nitrogen, the leaves turn pale and become sickly looking. However, if it's getting too much nitrogen (e.g., fertilizing your petunias with 30-10-10), you'll get a beautiful plant that looks a lot like lettuce but has few flowers. Phosphorus (down) stimulates the roots. Fertilizers with a high middle number are like espresso shots to freshly planted annuals, jump-starting the roots into vigorous growth. A 15-30-15 is a common flowering plant fertilizer because it keeps the plants blooming. Potassium (all-around) is the least understood but, in my opinion, the most important of the three elements. It's like a multivitamin for plants. It contains micronutrients such as iron, zinc, copper, sulphur and others that plants need in very small amounts just like we do. The best all-around inorganic fertilizer is 20-20-20 because of its high last number. Think of 20-20-20 as a balanced diet of all the food groups, whereas others, such as 10-52-10, are high fat, high caffeine, short term diets. I recommend 20-20-20 to keep annuals healthy all season.

The biggest disadvantages of inorganic fertilizers are that they are a short term fix and that, because you apply them via watering, a considerable amount of waste flows into the water table. If you plant an annual with a small root mass and douse it with a watering can full of 10-52-10, the tiny root system is going to catch only a tiny fraction of the phosphorus. This high degree of waste is making inorganics increasingly unpopular among environmentally aware gardeners. Excess inorganic fertilizer finds its way into waterways, lakes and eventually oceans, and along the way the high amounts of nitrates and phosphates are gobbled up by algae, allowing it to grow exponentially. Massive algae blooms will consume all available oxygen in a lake or pond, robbing aquatic plants and fish of oxygen and life. The result is a eutrophic water body, wherein there isn't enough oxygen to support a proper ecosystem. We need to avoid excessive fertilizer, even with our high octane annuals.

One solution to the above problem is to use slow-release pellets. We've found these very helpful at the greenhouse and sprinkle them in all of our hanging baskets. The tiny pellets contain the same inorganic fertilizer that you would normally mix with water, but they are trapped in a coating that slowly breaks down over a number of months so that the plant absorbs all the nutrients. Although this method doesn't deliver the "espresso shot" that the quick-release fertilizers do, it is lower maintenance and reduces the amount of chemicals flowing into our water bodies.

*Organic fertilizers:* these are fertilizers that are generally considered more environmentally friendly. Unfortunately for them they are also often composed of very unglamorous materials, such as slurry, worm castings, bat guano and manure. There is a massive selection of them, and it would take much more space than I have to describe them all (nor have I tried them all). Be wary of organic fertilizers that don't tell you what's in them. For a fertilizer to be federally approved it must list its active ingredient. If it doesn't, you may be buying snake oil.

I am usually very hesitant to recommend a particular fertilizer and will do so only after it has proven itself to me year after year. The only organic fertilizer that has done this for me is actually not technically a fertilizer at all, but a growth supplement called MYKE. MYKE is short for mycorrhizae, which is a naturally occurring fungus that has been around almost as long as plants themselves. The fungus attaches itself to the roots of plants and forms a symbiotic relationship with the root system: the fungus gets a home and nutrients, and in return, its long strands increase the surface area of the plant's roots. Root systems are like human brains; the more surface area they have, the more efficient they are. By increasing the surface area of the roots, the mycorrhizae fungus benefits the plant in the following ways:

- the roots are more efficient in capturing more of the moisture available, which in turn makes the plant more drought tolerant and increases its overall health
- the plant is able to use more nutrients from the inorganic fertilizers it is given, decreasing the waste and run-off
- a larger root system leads to a larger, more robust plant with larger, more numerous flowers, vegetables and fruit.

Sprinkle some MYKE in the hole before you plant to make sure it comes into direct contact with the roots.

The product MYKE is simply the mycorrhizae fungus in a dormant state. You apply it by sprinkling it in the planting hole so that it's in direct contact with the root system. It has to be applied at the time of planting, or it won't find the roots. MYKE isn't as fast acting as an inorganic fertilizer, and it takes about six weeks before you start to see the effects, but it will result in a much healthier plant overall. The only thing to remember about MYKE is that high concentrations of phosphorus are lethal to it; the phosphorus will burn the fungus. After applying MYKE, don't fertilize your plant with an inorganic fertilizer with a middle number higher than 20 (20-20-20 is fine). After a while you can probably get away with a middle number of 30, but don't use 10-52-10 at all.

I had the privilege of touring Premier Tech, the Quebec-based company that produces MYKE, and was impressed at the depth of the science that is behind it. At Salisbury we've been using and recommending it for the last few years and have been consistently and reliably impressed by its effects.

 means that the annual is a light feeder and requires very little fertilizer. I would add MYKE when you plant it and sprinkle a small amount of slow-release pellets on the soil. These annuals are the easiest to fertilize but also tend to be the slowest growing.

means that the plant needs an average amount of fertilizer. I recommend adding MYKE when you plant it, along with a generous sprinkle of slow-release pellets. In addition, feed it monthly with a full dose of 20-20-20. If the plant starts to look pale, increase the feeding to every two weeks.

is for annuals that are heavy feeders and require a lot of fertilizer. This category includes many of the high performance annuals that are the most popular. Add MYKE to the planting hole and sprinkle slow-release pellets on the surface of the soil when you plant them. They will also need a feeding of 20-20-20 once or twice a week. During their peak growing times in summer (at least a month after planting), you may want to switch to 15-30-15 to keep them blooming and beautiful. Even though they are heavy feeders, don't mix your fertilizer stronger than it indicates on the package or you're throwing money away and could damage your plant. Rich green leaves and robust stems mean that the plant is getting enough food.

Most Asked Question #5:
Compatibility
When I was a teenager I inherited a second-hand, 30-gallon fish tank. I was giddy because I'd always wanted a soothing tropical fish tank, so I hurried to the pet store to spend all my money. Thinking that a fish is a fish is a fish, I pretty much bought a wide assortment of whatever caught my eye, including a lot of neon tetras and a band of barbs. I went to sleep that night excited that I finally had a fish tank to call my own, so you can imagine the horror when I woke up the next morning to find the tank full of shredded tetra bits and some barbs that looked exceedingly pleased with themselves. The barbs, an aggressive fish, had made short work of the passive tetras.

Looking back, I realize that I violated the cardinal rule of fish tanks: don't put nasty fish in a closed space with nice fish. When you're planting annuals, and especially when you're container gardening, think of your container as a fish tank. It's an enclosed space where different species, with different evolutionary backgrounds and learned behaviours, battle each other for control of needed sunlight and precious little water and nutrients. Within every beautiful summer container on a patio, there's a merciless life or death struggle being waged.

The most beautiful containers, like the ones you see in magazines and on websites, pulse with tension because the competitors are so crammed in that each is trying desperately to get a leaf over the other's leaf. Before you buy your container stuffers, find out which plants go with which. A lot of people have spent a lot of money and time on containers that look great for only a few weeks until the dominant plant gobbles up the others.

Look carefully for the New Guinea impatiens being devoured by the "shark" nepeta vine.

Each plant in this book will have one of three symbols to tell you how aggressive it's going to be. You don't have to put just plants with the same symbol in each container, but think of the symbols as the fish store salesman who I wish had said to me, "I think I should tell you what will happen if you put those together." If you mix plants with different compatibilities, you will just need to be a little vigilant of protecting the passive plants—which is easy to do because, almost always, the more aggressive a plant is the easier it is to cut back. That being said, sometimes it's fun just to put a lot of plants in a container and watch them battle it out! The symbols are all fish based, in memory of my poor little tetras who never had a chance.

 Goldfish are passive annuals that grow slowly or sometimes barely at all. They include many of the most unorthodox annuals in this book, such as succulents, crotons and bromeliads. Often they're plants that are traditionally found inside the house, and sometimes they more expensive than other annuals; they tend to be the annuals that you'd want to keep year after year. Aggressive annuals will gobble them up quickly and gleefully, so it's important that you protect them. If you plant goldfish with sharks, keep the clippers handy so you can rescue the goldfish!

Trout are middle-of-the-road aggressive. They will fight for their share of space but aren't out for world domination. In an unsupervised fight against a shark they will lose, just as they will eventually begin muscling a goldfish out of their way.

 Sharks cover many of the most popular and fast growing container stuffers introduced in the last 10 years; these annuals are just plain imperialistic and will grow quickly in an attempt to control as much space as possible. They include annuals that grow the fastest, from trailing petunias to several vines; often they are the showiest braggarts available.

## The Pot-Drop: The Easiest Way to Keep an Annual Year After Year

In container gardening, we must often be innovative in order to turn our imagination into reality. A lot of the plants in this book break the rules of traditional gardening. It's unorthodox to bring houseplants and cacti outside and put them into a patio container, but I've always believed that gardeners make the rules, and gardeners can always

break them. Blending houseplants into containers full of annuals does have its hazards, however. They are often passive goldfish (see above), which don't do well in the survival-of-the-fittest environment of a container. They are also often fairly expensive because they are sold as plants that are meant to be kept for years on end.

When you're bringing inside plants outside for summer, I recommend "pot-dropping" them into your outside container instead of transplanting them from one pot to another. To pot-drop, simply dig a hole in the container that is the size of your plant's indoor pot, plunk it in and backfill it to hide the pot. The plant's roots (often delicate) are protected from other aggressive annuals, and it is easy to bring the plant back indoors when the season is over. It also allows you to have plants with different moisture requirements in the same container because you have two enclosed spaces. For example, you could pot-drop a large succulent, which likes life on the dry side, into a container with bacopa and alocasia, which need more moisture. In autumn, dig up the pot, wash it off, usually give the plant some safe soap to get rid of any pests that may try to hitchhike inside, and you can bring it indoors until next spring.

In putting this anthurium with a much more aggressive 'Diamond Frost' euphorbia, I'm making sure to protect the former because I want to bring it inside over winter.

You can also use this technique if you want to have plants that need a different medium, such as orchids, in a mixed container, or if you're using plants that bloom only for a short time and then need to be replaced, such as flowering houseplants.

## A Word About Choosing Healthy Plants

You can't have a healthy garden with unhealthy plants. Just as savvy grocery shoppers know to buy bread at one store and meat at another, many gardeners hop from one garden centre to the other during the few frantic, sunny weekends in May, gathering their various favourites along the way. Spotting the perfect annual is as much an art form as choosing the perfect cantaloupe, and like the cantaloupe, there are tell-tale signs as to whether or not an annual will thrive in your garden.

When choosing your annuals, the first thing to decide is where to go first. In the spring gardening world, there are independent garden centres and there are box stores. The artificial choice that many gardeners believe they have is to go to one if they want quality and the other if they want low prices. That is often but not always true. Savvy gardeners who are at a box store the day the truck arrives with fresh plants often find pitch-perfect quality, and many independents, including my own, are learning not to be afraid of deep discounts and are challenging the boxes at their own game. There are also things that independents offer that

the boxes, though they keep trying, just haven't been able to match—staff expertise, selection and the proper environment for keeping plants healthy.

The way I look at it, there are many things in life that are a chore to buy; plants shouldn't be one of them. Shopping for your plants sets the tone for the whole gardening season. In some ways it is the most important part of the gardening season; it's where you meet the plants that will share your yard with you, the plants you'll nurture and grow and that will brag and perform for you. When our customers come through the door in

Annuals are like pies; the best ones are always homemade.

spring, it's always with big, wide eyes and a head full of ideas and possibilities. Buying gas is a chore, so it makes sense that you buy your gas at the cheapest place—period. Gardening is about discovery, creativity and fulfilment. To me, it makes sense that you buy your plants at a place where those things matter. It also helps to have confidence that the plants you're buying and are going to invest your time and energy into are healthy, and to be able to talk to people who know about what would look good with what and what will do well where.

In choosing the perfect plant, whether you shop at an independent garden centre or a box store, you should know that the health of an annual is more than skin (or in this case, flower) deep. It's common for first-time gardeners to choose the plant with the most wide open flowers, only to be disappointed when it's finished blooming and has nothing left to give. Look at the overall shape of a plant. Make sure your plant is full bodied and not too leggy. Don't fall for the old in-full-bloom-but-no-leaves trick. Open flowers are good; healthy buds are better; a full, lush plant with healthy leaves and a strong stem is best. Don't be shy about checking the roots by tipping the pot over (supporting the plant, of course) and tapping the bottom. It can damage a plant to just yank it out by the stem. You're typically looking for a well-colonized rootball with a nice balance of thick (tuberous) and fibrous roots. If chunks of soil fall away, the pot is too large, and if you have trouble removing it from the pot, it's rootbound. Usually the roots should be white, though colour can vary with species. If the colour of the leaves appears pale and/or the

Don't be afraid to carefully check a plant's root system if you suspect that it's not healthy.

main stem is weak and floppy, the plant is either not getting enough fertilizer or was grown in temperatures that were too warm (which industrial growers will sometimes do to put out a quick crop). Check it for weeds; any weeds in the pot could spread to your container or flower bed. If the plant is strong and well-branched and its roots are healthy, then any open blooms are a bonus! At a good garden centre, you should be able to get the whole, healthy package, flowers and all.

Once you've bought your healthy plant, make sure it gets a good start. If you like to get your plants early (because some of the most talked about annuals do sell out quickly), it's important that they get some time outside even if they aren't planted yet. I always suggest keeping them in a wheelbarrow so that it's easy to push them outside if it's going to be a warm day and pull them inside if it's going to freeze. Outdoor plants need the sunshine and the elements of the outdoors; otherwise, they will go downhill quickly.

## Pests and Solutions

No book about annuals can be complete without a word about what can go wrong with them. Following are some of the most common afflictions that annuals get. This list is by no means exhaustive, and I don't include pests and diseases that typically afflict larger plants and perennials. The types of pest that might afflict your garden depend on the type of growing season we are having.

When it comes to controlling pests, it's an understatement to say that using poisonous chemicals should be a last resort. The John Wayne mentality of nuking everything annoying in our yard is, thankfully, passing away with many other unfortunate 20th-century habits. If you feel you must use poisons in your yard, please take the following into consideration.

• If you can't see it, you can't kill it with a chemical. Systemics, which poison the insides of the plant and turn it into a poison apple for anything feeding on it, are long banned because of their tendency to cause cancer. If the spray doesn't come into direct contact with the critter, it won't work, which in itself means that chemicals are very rarely truly effective. Every day I have tell customers that, because chemical "X" is off the market, the only action they can take is preventative. Some people, especially those who have become accustomed to dousing their yards in poison at the first sign of insect life, don't like hearing that, but our habits need to change.

• Never, ever spray a plant when it's in bloom—that goes for everything from apple trees to annuals. Spraying a bloom will kill the pollinating insects, such as the once-common bumblebee. We must cherish and protect our remaining bees.

• If you're wondering if it's safe for your pet, your kids or you, the answer is no. A poison is always a poison; it's a question of degree. It kills little critters quickly, and it just takes longer for the big critters.

- There's a perception that if the active ingredient in a chemical is organic or natural, it is less toxic to humans. This perception is a myth—some of the deadliest toxins on earth are naturally occurring.
- Always follow the instructions on the container. Chemicals are like antibiotics; using too little will result in the attacker surviving to become immune, and using too much will cause damage to you and your environment. The reason that many systemic chemicals were pulled off the market was that people were using them in reckless ways; if we continue to apply chemicals recklessly, they will all be taken away.

Never spray a tree in bloom or you'll kill bees, which are becoming alarmingly rare.

I'll come down off my soapbox now. Here are some of the various pests you might run into and how you can deal with them.

*Ants:* the first thing to ask yourself when you see ants in your yard is, "Are they doing any damage?" If the answer is no, I say live and let live. They actually remove a lot of unwanted fungi and bacteria from the soil and reduce the rate of disease in the long term. If they move into your flower bed, however, there are ways to get rid of them. You can control them by soaking their nest every time you water. If that doesn't work, take a shovel and scoop up the nest to expose as much of the inner nesting chambers as possible (and ideally the queen). Pour in a pot of boiling water and they should get the hint. A product called diatomaceous earth also works well. Sprinkle it around the ant hill, and they will be unable to crawl over it; think of it as razor wire for ants (wear a mask when you apply it so you don't breathe it in). It won't kill the ants, but they will move on. *Note:* if ants move into your house, forget live-and-let-live, as they can do a lot of damage. Call a professional right away.

*Aphids:* ah, yes, the evil aphid. Many people are surprised to learn how many sizes, colours and even textures they come in, with over 4400 species identified worldwide! They can afflict almost anything and are instantly recognizable, huddling in the hundreds around new growth.

Aphids

A few aphids are common, and often predators are not far behind to keep the aphids in line. They are the jelly doughnuts of the insect world; almost everything loves to eat them (except ants, which actually live symbiotically with aphids, and if ants are on you're plant it's a good indication there are aphids nearby). If their populations outgrow natural predatory control, they can do a lot of damage by sucking the fluid out of your leaves. The most effective predators are ladybugs and spiders (so never kill spiders in your yard). More and more garden centres now sell packs of ladybugs, which are well worth it. You can also douse the plant in insecticidal soap, which is essentially soapy water. In late summer, clouds of migrating aphids wreak havoc on picnics and porches everywhere. If your annual comes

Ladybug

down with a bad case of them after the end of August, I usually recommend throwing in the towel. By the end of the season, annuals' immune systems are so tired that they can't effectively fight pests off, so the aphids will just keep coming.

*Spider mites:* spider mites are nasty critters that are smaller and harder to see than aphids. Look for tell-tale fine webbing around the new growth of a plant. They tend to afflict plants that are heat and/or water stressed. A strong jet of water now and then will keep them at bay; if they persist, try insecticidal soap.

*Fungus gnats:* these gnats are the little flies that live in wet soil and like to fly up into your face. They are harmless to plants (unless it's a small seedling) and humans. They are feeding on assorted organic detritus on top of or in the soil and thrive in perpetually moist conditions. They can come from a number of places, including being imported on a plant that has been consistently overwatered in the store. To get rid of them, hang some yellow sticky-strips around the base of the plant. They can't resist yellow. Dry out the top of the plant and scrape off the top layer of soil, depriving the gnats of their home and food source, and replace it with good stuff. The adults live only a week or two, so without a suitable home they'll be gone soon.

*Slugs:* yech! During a cool, damp summer, slugs can be a menace to many plants in your garden. They live in moist, heavily shaded areas, with the best real estate being amongst rotting leaves and other nasty bits of detritus. They come out at night and take big chomps out of the leaves of annuals and perennials, usually leaving a tell-tale trail of dried slime behind for you to find in the morning. Fortunately, they are relatively easy to get rid of. I find that the most effective way is to lay a margarine container lid (or something of about equal depth) in the soil with beer in it. The rim has to be low enough that they can crawl in. They love beer—they are attracted to the yeast—and will get drunk and drown in their own debauchery. Copper wire or ribbon also works well; it delivers a kind of electric shock to the slimy critters, and they can't crawl across it. The downside here is that to protect all your plants, you'll need a lot of copper, and it may look unsightly in the garden. Just before the snow flies in autumn, check in the dampest, shadiest places of the garden for their eggs, which look like caviar. Clean them up so that there will be fewer slugs to worry about the next season.

Slug

Spittle bugs

*Spittle bugs:* if it looks like the neighbourhood kids have been spitting in your garden, you probably have spittle bugs. The spittle is actually a foamy protective coating covering the animal itself, which is a tiny, orange dot. This coating is very effective and renders most sprays ineffective. It's easy to get rid of them, however, by washing them away with a good high pressure shot from the hose.

*Powdery mildew:* in 300 AD, the Greeks wrote about white fungal splotches affecting their rose bushes—some things never change! During cloudy, damp periods, many gardeners will notice white circles appearing on their plants. Powdery mildew affects some plants, such as roses, phlox, begonias and lawn, more than others. It occurs when the leaves stay wet and cool and don't have sufficient air circulation to dry out. You can help prevent powdery mildew by cleaning up autumn leaves from your flower beds; some of these leaves can carry the fungus through winter and infect plants in spring, especially if

used as mulch. If you see powdery mildew on your annuals, cut back on the watering if you can and try to water only in the mornings. Trim some lower leaves off to encourage air circulation. If these steps fail, you can sprinkle some sulphur, sold at any garden centre, on the affected leaves.

Now that I've bored you with the basics (if you made it through all of that, you really are keen for gardening), we can move on to the fun stuff. Remember that planting annuals isn't a chore; it's the farthest thing from labouring in the fields. The gardening I love is all about creativity and inspiration, and I hope that the wonderful plants in the pages that follow inspire you just as much as they have inspired me. Good growing and have fun!

Powdery mildew

# Abutilon

Botanical Name: *Abutilon* x *hybridum*
Aliases: flowering maple, Indian mallow, parlour maple

**Height:** 30–40 cm • **Spread:** 35–45 cm

There are two kinds of gardeners: those who love abutilon and those who haven't discovered it yet! The tree-form abutilon, flowering maple, has been a semi-popular houseplant for years, with adventurous gardeners putting it in a container as a specimen on a patio. Now there is a miniature version that grows to only about 30 cm tall and blooms little pastel satellite dishes like crazy! This plant definitely receives one of my "Least-Appreciated" awards.

**The Basics:** From the large Mallow family, abutilon is widespread throughout the subtropical regions of the world and likes consistently moist soil, so keep it well watered. Although the tag might say "full sun," I would protect it in the afternoon (especially on the Prairies) by positioning it in strong partial sun—morning with dappled afternoon is best. Fading or burnt leaves indicate too much direct sun. Keep it fertilized and it should bloom almost continuously all summer with minimal deadheading.

The old-fashioned flowering maple standard.

**Recommended Varieties:**
**'Bella'** is an ultra compact, prolifically flowering version of the larger, often gangly original and came out several years ago. I was very impressed. It daubs a mound of rich pastels into containers, with flowers that are only slightly more muted than hibiscus but the same shape. There are other varieties that are good as well; just make sure your plant is bushy with rich green leaves (a sign that it has been fertilized properly).

**Things to Know:** Watch for whiteflies and aphids.

'Bella' looks great in a simple container with green dichondra.

**Best Uses:** Abutilon is an ideal centrepiece in a smallish (less than 40 cm across) container. Its colouring is a unique splash of pastels that goes well with either woodsy accents, such as ferns or English ivy, or tropical foliage. If you have a sheltered sanctuary in the backyard or on the patio, this is a good plant to sit on a little table next to your seat. It's a true dwarf and is so compact that it can even be used in hanging baskets with some tropical vines or bacopa.

# Ageratum

Botanical Name: *Ageratum houstonianum*
Aliases: floss flower, whiteweed

**Height:** to 25 cm • **Spread:** to 50 cm

For years, old-fashioned floss flower has been popular for borders and accents but has never earned the spotlight because it wasn't all that vigorous. Now the next generation of ageratum is vigorous and free-flowering enough to be the star! Its unique flossy texture and mushrooming mounds of colour make it well worth trying in your containers.

**The Basics:** Ageratum loves the sun but not the heat, so try moving it into some afternoon shade once summer sets in. It prefers moist soil and tends to pout and shed its blooms if it dries out. Once the flush of flowers is getting tired, you can speed up the next flush by giving it a light haircut and some fertilizer.

**Recommended Varieties:** The **Artist Series** are reliable plants that explode into fuzzy clumps of blues, purples or pinks in May and June. Like all ageratums, these perform best before summer gets too warm, but you can extend their performance by providing afternoon shelter and ample water. I recommend seed-grown ageratums, like the classic **Hawaii Series**, for flower beds or mass plantings. You can usually find these in four- or six-packs.

The purples and pinks of 'Artist Purple' with 'Sunsatia' nemesia make a perfect summer basket.

**Best Uses:** Ageratum is very compact and pairs well with similar habits. Try pairing it with a Soprano Series osteospermum for a beautiful combination of blues. It will also pair well with container-mates that don't want to dry out, such as bacopa and diascia. These three together are one of my favourite small hanging basket mixes in spring. Artist ageratums tolerate heat better than many others; try matching them with other early-season beauties, such as violas.

**Things to Know:** If you plant ageratum in full sun, make sure that you keep it well watered whenever it's blooming. It reacts to drying out much like bacopa: the flowers dry up and don't appear again for a couple of weeks.

Thanks to its compact habit, the Artist Series looks great planted alone.

# Alstroemeria

Botanical Name: *Alstroemeria aurantiaca*
Aliases: princess lily, Peruvian lily, lily of the Incas, parrot lily

**Height:** 1 m · **Spread:** to 60 cm

Alstroemeria grows wild in the cool altitude of the Andes and is a common sight on the trail to Machu Picchu. I always recommend this one as a great Mother's Day gift. It is usually expensive because it takes a long time to mature, but the customers I've talked to who have purchased one have said it's well worth it—it sits in the container, minds its own business and blooms like crazy.

**The Basics:** I'd recommend that you plant princess lilies in the ground instead of in containers, the reason being that they are a bit fussy about root temperature and tend to stop blooming when the soil gets too warm. Soil raised above the ground in containers receives lateral warming from the sun unless it's in the shade. Keeping the roots in the cool earth will keep the plant blooming longer. Keep the soil moist whenever this plant is blooming.

**Recommended Varieties:** Dwarf varieties are relatively new to the Canadian market and have become popular very quickly. The flowers will look familiar; it's the same genus as the alstroemeria that is famous as a cut flower, only those plants grow up to 3 m tall. **'Princess'** is the most popular dwarf variety and is an early-season favourite that thrives in cool temperatures. It blooms longer than other alstroemerias because it is sterile and doesn't go to seed. It is a bit too dwarf for cut flowers, but the cuts are easy enough to find in flower shops.

'Princess Isabella' is a fiery orange and yellow bicolour.

**Best Uses:** Plant it alongside a path that you walk along often because every time you look at a princess lily in bloom, your day will get a little bit brighter. One of my neighbours had some simple pots of alstroemeria outside her front door, and the flowers bloomed for months.

**Things to Know:** Alstroemeria rhizomes are notoriously invasive in the wild, so when planting, give them some space, and if you're putting them in containers, try them on their own. Don't worry, one alstroemeria will give off quite a display!

'Princess Susana' is a delicate blush colour with black whiskers.

# Begonia—Tuberous

**Botanical Name:** *Begonia* x *tuberhybrida*

**Height:** to 50 cm • **Spread:** to 50 cm

It's a biological wonder how begonias bring such a baffling amount of brightness and vibrancy into the shadiest nooks and crannies of the garden. They are a very diverse genus hailing mostly from South American jungles, where they grow in the dappled light of the jungle floor. There are many varieties and many uses, but here I'm focusing on the varieties most popular for Canadian gardeners.

**The Basics:** Nothing beats begonia's blast of bright, classic colours in the shadows. Remove the single, female flowers when they appear, leaving only the double, male flowers to keep the plant blooming. Let it dry out slightly between waterings, and try not to water the foliage, especially in the cool evening.

**Recommended Varieties:** The fact that there's nothing new about tuberous begonias is a testament to how fabulous the old-fashioned varieties are. For sheer colour, I recommend the **Non-Stop Series**, which performs so well that it is usually easy to find. Vibrant, primary reds and yellows are like flashlights cutting through the shade. **'Mocca'** is a type of Non-Stop with rich, chocolate brown foliage that highlights the vibrant blooms nicely.

**'Solenia'** is a fairly new introduction of begonias bred to grow in the sun. The flowers are rosettes and smaller than Non-Stops, and the plant keeps a pleasing compact habit. It has dark, glossy leaves and performs well in partial to full sun, though it may need some protection in the afternoon.

If you fancy the larger-flowering begonias (the **Belgiums**), they are available either as a bulb in February to start in pots or, sometimes, as finished plants in larger garden centres. Larger garden centres often carry the larger begonias, often with stunning ruffled or picotee blooms. The American bulbs are usually the most exotic, while the Belgium bulbs are the largest.

**Best Uses:** Non-Stops are versatile enough to be used in almost any shady area, whether it's a flower bed or a container. I personally prefer to fill the shady flower beds with single impatiens and keep the Non-Stop begonias in containers because they aren't as prone to powdery mildew when raised off the ground. 'Solenia' has a robust tropical look that blends well with other dark annuals such as alocasia and 'Blackie' sweet potato vine. The larger begonias are striking in a container. My mother often fills a whiskey barrel with them at her shady back door, and they look fabulous.

'Mocca's' dark leaves provide sharp contrast.

The charming rosettes of 'Solenia' have increasing sun tolerance.

Ruffled begonias are hard to find but worth it.

**Things to Know:** The perennial problem with begonias is watering. If you don't let them dry out a little bit between waterings, they may develop powdery mildew or an unsightly black slime could form on the soil. Make sure there is ample air circulation (admittedly difficult sometimes in sheltered areas). Keep the base of the plant free of old and rotting leaves to help keep the air flowing and mildew at bay.

**Overwintering Bulbs:** Overwintering begonias is worth it because over summer they store energy in their bulbs, which leads to a stronger, more robust plant with

Pinch off the single flowers (left) so your begonia doesn't go to seed.

'Non-Stop Pink' is a vibrant, almost hot pink that really draws attention to itself.

bigger blooms the next spring. To overwinter, snip off the main stem at ground level once it turns yellow or after the foliage has died off from a gentle frost (a hard frost of -4° C or more will damage the tuber). Lift out the tuber and snip off the remainder of the stem. Clean all soil and debris carefully off and dry it well. It's important that the tuber is very dry. Store it in dry peat moss or wood shavings in a cool dark place (a root cellar is perfect) until early spring, when you can plant it in a window pot until it's ready to go outside. These instructions are basically the same for many other annuals that can be overwintered.

# Black-Eyed Susan

**Botanical Name:** *Rudbeckia hirta*
Aliases: coneflower, gloriosa daisy, yellow ox-eye daisy

**Height:** 10 cm–1 m • **Spread:** 10–50 cm

Black-eyed Susan, with its simple yellow cheerfulness and hardy disposition, has long been a favourite perennial. It's a workhorse of a flower, producing a mass of colour under the summer sun. It is very versatile, performing well in anything from mass plantings to container gardens, and it will bring its cheerful flowers wherever you put it. The downside to black-eyed Susan is that it doesn't bloom until the summer days are long and warm, and its foliage isn't very attractive.

'Cherry Brandy' is the darkest black-eyed Susan.

**The Basics:** Black-eyed Susans love full sun and are fairly drought tolerant. They also love the wind, so make sure they have lots of air circulation around them. Don't over-fertilize them or they may develop weak stems.

**Recommended Varieties:** These are exciting plants because new colours and cultivars keep coming out with no decrease in performance; the new varieties work as hard as their traditional country cousins, so I'm often discovering a new favourite! I love the **Toto Series**. It's dwarf (about 20 cm tall) and is the first to bloom, exploding into stout mushrooms of yellow and orange. For mid-sized, I like **'Sonora'** (to 50 cm tall) because even though its size and big, bicoloured flowers make it suitable for larger containers, it maintains an attractive, compact shape. I like **'Irish Spring'** (to 80 cm tall) for its hint of orange and cheeky green eye, and **'Prairie Sun'** (to 90 cm tall) for its sheer volume of colour. I tend to stay away from the double-flowering types, like **'Cherokee Sunset,'** because I find the foliage a bit too messy.

**Best Uses:** The dwarf varieties, such as **'Becky'** and **'Toto,'** are great in smaller containers or window boxes. Use the larger varieties, like the red **'Cherry Brandy'** and **'Irish Eyes,'** in a very large container (I'm talking whiskey barrel size) or as no effort, high performance show-offs in the flower bed. When planting the larger species, in either a bed or a container, put smaller plants around them to disguise black-eyed Susan's somewhat floppy foliage. **'Tiger Eyes'** is the first hybrid that I would use alone in a container. For a burst of summer colour, plant the tallest variety in the centre of a container and work down to dwarfs on the sides (maybe with some bidens for a trailer). They are some of the best flowers for attracting bees and birds to your garden. Tall black-eyed Susans last a long time as cut flowers.

**Things to Know:** In humid regions watch for powdery mildew, especially if the plants are too close together or in a sheltered area. The leaves have a coarse, peach-fuzzy texture that might irritate sensitive skin.

'Cherokee Sunset' boasts large, double flowers.

# Cobbity Daisy

**Botanical Name:** *Argyranthemum frutescens*
Aliases: Marguerite daisy, dill daisy, Paris daisy

**Height:** to 50 cm • **Spread:** to 40 cm

Daisies are one of the most universally classic and beloved garden flowers, but there are so many different types that it can get confusing. Cobbity daisies are quickly becoming *the* daisy to use. They originally grew only in the Canary Islands but have been hybridized into a very versatile container stuffer. These daisies require little maintenance, bloom like crazy and fill every container they're in with the simple summer beauty that only daisies have.

**The Basics:** Cobbities have a classic large, bell-shaped growth habit. A well-branched plant shouldn't need any more pinching to acquire a full shape. These daisies need well-drained soil and don't like wet feet; they are slightly drought tolerant. They are sun lovers, and while they will tolerate some shade, too much will result in fewer flowers and spindly branches.

**Recommended Varieties:** 'Butterfly' is my favourite. If you're in a sour mood, take one look at its audacious display of vibrant yellow and you'll find yourself trying to remember what all the fuss was about! **'Sunlight'** is also a fabulous yellow. Once you start moving from yellows and pinks into reds and doubles, the plants tend to be smaller and bloom a bit less, which might be all right if you have a smaller container. Single white cobbities are often larger plants than their yellow cousins, so while they may be too large for containers, they are perfect for a traditional cottage theme.

**Best Uses:** Use yellow or pink cobbities to brighten up larger containers (40 cm or more across) where the goal is colour and lots of it. A variety like 'Butterfly' is large enough to be a centrepiece but will benefit from a vertical accent such as curly willow or a canna lily.

**Things to Know:** This plant might tucker out in the heat of summer, but don't fret. Instead of forcing it to bloom during a heat wave, give

Double cobbities don't bloom as much but are beautiful when they do.

it a generous haircut and fertilize it well. You'll thank yourself when it comes back with renewed vigour once the weather cools off.

Keep cobbities trimmed if you want a compact growth habit.

# Crown of Thorns

Botanical Name: *Euphorbia milii*
Aliases: Christ plant, Siamese lucky plant

**Height:** 45–60 cm • **Spread:** 45–60 cm

I remember being on a motorboat somewhere through the floating villages of the Mekong Delta and seeing a crown of thorns in the window of many one-room floating homes/boats. That was a lesson for me in the importance of gardening in people's lives: no matter how poor people are, they will find a way to make something grow. When I see these striking red and peach flowers, I'm reminded of that fact.

Look for robust plants when you're shopping.

**The Basics:** This plant is a native of Madagascar that has long been a semi-popular houseplant and is now becoming trendy in container gardening. The reason for this popularity, other than its vibrant colour, is that there are precious few other colourful annuals that will tolerate very hot and dry conditions. You'll find that it will become leggy as it matures; this is normal—its habit is naturally prostrate.

**Recommended Varieties:** Crown of thorns is still a bit of a rarity, so you may need to call some larger garden centres before you find it. Red is the most popular colour, but you may be able to find it in peach or apricot; there are actually dozens of cultivars. Look for the most compact plant.

**Best Uses:** This plant is perfect for hot, hot planters and should be paired with other heat lovers that like life on the dry side, such as portulaca or succulents. The hotter it is, the better it will do. Unlike cactus, however, it likes some humidity with its heat, so if you have a water feature on an exposed, sunny deck, the perfect place for crown of thorns is right next to it. It's very slow growing and makes a great plant to bring inside for winter.

**Things to Know:** Crown of thorns isn't always easy to find and has usually been brought in from Florida or California. It doesn't transport well and usually comes off the truck defoliated and needs several weeks before it is beautiful again. Make sure you get a healthy one, but don't worry too much if it's missing some leaves; they'll come back with lots of light and heat. The milky sap is poisonous, so wear gloves when pruning this plant. The thorns, of course, are very sharp.

Unlike what the name implies, this is not the plant the Romans put on Christ's head. That is thought to be *Paliurus spina-christi*, which is native to Jerusalem.

As they mature, crown of thorns lose much of their cuteness.

# Dahlia

Botanical Name: *Dahlia* x *hybrida*

**Height:** 30–90 cm or more • **Spread:** to 30 cm

Native to Mexico, dahlias are one of the most universally loved flowers in the garden. Different sizes of dahlia typically fill different roles in the garden. When people think of dahlias it is often of large, sunflower-like flowers standing 90 cm or more tall. These are flower bed classics, but it is the relatively new varieties of dwarf dahlias, ideal for container gardens, that have made the biggest recent impact.

**The Basics:** Dahlia size ranges from the looming dinner plates to the clumping dwarfs that usually don't exceed 30 cm tall. They are very versatile, loving the sun but able to tolerate some shade. Give them ample fertilizer and well-drained soil and they will perform joyously all summer!

**Recommended Varieties:** I recommend starting the larger decorative or dinner-plate varieties from bulbs on your windowsill in April. My favourite decorative dahlia is the sublime **'Arabian Night.'** Smaller, more compact dahlias are now the dahlia of choice for many gardeners because of their container-friendly habit and their constant blooming. The **Dahlietta Series** is excellent (it's the one where all the colours have female names, like **'Lauren'**). The **Figaro Series** is wonderful; it has big, plum-sized blooms throughout summer, and its pure, simple colours make it perfect in any size of container. If you want a more exotic-looking flower, the **Goldalia Series** offers a few bicolours. **'Fireworks'** promises to be the first striped dahlia.

**Best Uses:** The big dahlias are eye-catchers in the flower bed, especially against a wall or a fence. They may also work in a very large container. Dwarf dahlias are perfect for containers. Their tolerance of a range of conditions makes them ideal container-mates for almost anything. Try them alternated between sweet potato vines, or match them with 'Diamond Frost' euphorbia and

Burgundy Dahliettas have a beautiful richness.

'Figaro Pink' is a soft yet vibrant pink.

Larger dahlias are best for the garden where they can show off.

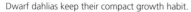
Dwarf dahlias keep their compact growth habit.

enjoy the contrast of the big, colourful dahlia flowers with the lace-like, white euphorbia flowers.

**Things to Know:** If dahlias don't have proper air circulation and it's a cold, wet summer, watch for powdery mildew (white splotches) on the leaves. To treat mildew, make sure your plant has ample air circulation and thin out some of the lower leaves. Apply sulphur dust if necessary.

I love the richness of red dahlias.

Dwarf dahlias are compact enough for this mix with lobelias and Boston fern.

You can overwinter dahlia tubers (see Overwintering Bulbs, p. 48, for how), and you'll be rewarded with a healthier plant each year. Dahlia tubers are edible, and when they were first brought to Europe from the New World, it was thought that they would be an alternative to the potato.

# Dianthus

**Botanical Name:** *Dianthus barbatus*
Aliases: carnation, pink, sweet William

**Height:** to 40 cm · **Spread:** to 40 cm

Dianthus is also known as "pink" because it looks like it has been cut out with pinking shears. It has been a traditional favourite in Europe for centuries, and it will bring a familiar, cottage garden look to flower beds and containers. New varieties are not only increasingly vigorous and heat tolerant but also come in bewitchingly beautiful colours.

**The Basics:** Dianthus needs lots of sun to keep its colour rich and its habit compact. It likes well-drained soil that doesn't get too dry and will tolerate slightly alkaline (chalky) conditions. It won't perform well during a heat wave, but besides that it should bloom all summer. Dead-heading spent flowers before they set seed will help.

**Recommended Varieties:** There are a multitude of varieties available. The classic is **'Prince William'** ('Wee Willie'). It's small (15 cm tall tops) but blooms into a carpet of pinks and reds. **'Corona'** is a whimsical jester that blooms bright cherry, lavender or a swirling tie-dye of the two. With 'Corona,' the colour mosaic on each flower seems to be as unique as a fingerprint. My personal favourite is the **Parfait Series**, which comes in **'Strawberry,' 'Raspberry'** and **'Peppermint.'** The flowers on 'Raspberry' are a juicy red with rich wine centres.

**Best Uses:** Dianthus is ideal for mass plantings because of the mass of bright colour it produces. New varieties such as the Parfait Series and 'Corona' make great container stuffers, adding a unique colour splash when put between a trailer and a larger centrepiece. Dianthus is not a very aggressive plant, so avoid putting it next to high performance annuals such as trailing petunias and million bells. If you have an alkaline spot in the garden, try pairing it with baby's breath, zinnia or verbena; you could do the same in a container if you add a touch of lime to the potting mix.

Though it's not new, 'Prince William' is still one of my favourites.

**Things to Know:** Happily, dianthus doesn't attract many pests. Watch for powdery mildew in humid regions.

'Red Hot' is a new variety that offers bright red double flowers.

# Diascia

Botanical Name: *Diascia barberae*
Aliases: twin spur

**Height:** to 30 cm • **Spread:** to 30 cm

I don't use the term "adorable" very often, but this little plant is just plain adorable! Native to southern Africa, diascia is a recent gardening introduction but has become popular quickly thanks to its vivacious colours and its love affair with Canadian spring weather. A diascia in full bloom, bursting with saucy apricot and juicy strawberry colours, is hard to resist. Although it will melt in the summer heat, in spring it's a treat to have in the garden.

**The Basics:** Diascia loves the sun but prefers cooler temperatures, so try to give it some afternoon shade or dappled light. Like nemesia and pansies, it performs best in spring and autumn, when it's cooler. Pinching back old diascia flowers will help to promote new growth and keep it blooming. During summer, expect it to tucker out. The best thing is to give it a haircut and some fertilizer and enjoy your heat-loving annuals for a while. Keep it moist but not wet.

This charming basket of little flowers includes bacopa, nemesia and diascia.

**Recommended Varieties:** There are many varieties of diascia that either bunch or slightly trail. Look for plants that are well branched, and avoid them if they are pale or have only a few stringy stems; those will take more time to fill out. My favourite is one of the originals: **'Little Charmer'** is a compact, upright plant with a delightful growth habit. It is shorter than most varieties but has the largest, densest flowers. **'Wink'** is a compact form that also performs well. If you're sampling trailing types, two of the best are **'Flying Colors'** and **'Whisper.'**

**Best Uses:** 'Little Charmer' is the most compact variety, which makes it a perfect mix with spring lovers such as ageratum, bacopa or nemesia in a small container. Trailing varieties are larger and are best suited for mixed hanging baskets. Diascia also performs well in rock gardens, where it's likely to be the first colour of spring while the perennials are still groggy.

**Things to Know:** Diascia likes its space and air circulation; don't crowd it too tightly, or its leaves will stay wet and it may develop powdery mildew.

Trailing varieties have a more spreading habit.

# Euphorbia

Botanical Name: *Euphorbia hypericifolia* hybrid
Aliases: diamond frost

**Height:** to 45 cm • **Spread:** to 45 cm

I love this plant! The individually unremarkable flowers act as a collective, growing and repeatedly branching into a white cloud that drifts through your container, adding texture and sharply defining the shape and colour of the flowers emerging from it. Euphorbia is not only beautiful, but it also makes its container-mates more beautiful. Don't miss out on this one!

**The Basics:** Euphorbia is part of a massive family that includes poinsettias and many popular succulents. It loves hot weather (don't be afraid to put it in full sun) and will tolerate some drought. It is very low maintenance, and you don't need to deadhead it or cut it back for it to branch freely.

**Recommended Varieties:** **'Diamond Frost'** is the best and until recently probably the only variety. **'Pink Blush'** is a new variety that performs well, though it might not grow as large as the white variety. The pink is quite subtle and will contrast well with red or dark pink annuals. Given the massive popularity of 'Diamond Frost,' expect to see many more euphorbias out in the next few years.

**Best Uses:** No garden should be without some euphorbia! It's easy to grow, looks amazing and will fit into your design theme whether you want a modern or a classic look. Try pairing it with bold-bloomed annuals such as osteospermums, dahlias or geraniums, which will look like crisp mountain peaks rising out of a cloud of euphorbia. For a contemporary look pair it with purple fountain grass, which will arc out of the euphorbia, or with a simple vertical curly willow accent. You can also use euphorbia at Christmas to pair with poinsettias; it works fairly well, though euphorbia is an item that you will have to buy at a garden centre (usually only a larger one) and won't be able to grow yourself.

Its habit is both airy and compact; it achieves the best of both worlds.

**Things to Know:** The white sap of euphorbia is a skin irritant, so if you're cutting it back, wear gloves or wash your hands afterward.

'Pink Blush' looks great with red million bells.

# Gazania

Botanical Name: *Gazania rigens*
Aliases: treasure flower

**Height:** to 25 cm • **Spread:** to 25 cm

I've never seen a flower brighter than a gazania. It's the perfect sun-loving show-stopper and is becoming more popular every year as more gardeners look for drought- and heat-tolerant annuals. Gazania is easy to grow, and when the sun comes out the plant unfurls flowers that radiate colour and have such startlingly precise symmetrical patterns that they will hold your eye like a hypnotic swirl. If you have a hot spot in your yard, plant a gazania.

**The Basics:** This South African native loves heat above all things. It tolerates drought and will grow in gritty or sandy soil. Deadheading gazania after it is done blooming will promote new flowers, but be careful while doing it because the spent flowers look a lot like the unopened buds.

**Recommended Varieties:** I find the **Kiss Series** (to 20 cm tall) to have the most vibrant colours, and the flowers are often the earliest to bloom. The flowers also boast strikingly crisp symmetry that will catch your eye and usually hold it for a while. **'Big Kiss'** (to 25 cm tall) promises to have the same vibrant colour as the original but with larger (11 cm across) flowers on fuller plants.

**Best Uses:** Gazania is one of the best solutions for the hot sun and performs at its best when the mercury rises to almost 30° C. If you've been looking for something to fill that western exposure, right under the white siding that reflects the heat, then mix gazania with 'Diamond Frost' euphorbia and watch them celebrate. Gazania loves sun so much that on cloudy, dreary days it will close its flowers and just stay in bed all day. It will provide great colour in a container with Australian annuals such as talinum and flambe. You can plant it in the ground but, as the soil will inevitably be cooler, it won't grow with the same vigour as in a raised container. Be wary of pairing gazania with a sun lover that has to stay moist, such as petunia or ageratum.

Gazania keeps its compact habit and doesn't need to be trimmed back.

**Things to Know:** Don't plant gazania too soon or the cold nights will stunt its growth. Be careful not to overwater it.

This gazania looks brilliant paired with harmonic orange and burgundy.

# Heliotrope

Botanical Name: *Heliotropium arborescens*
Aliases: cherry pie, turnsole, common heliotrope, Peruvian
   heliotrope

**Height:** to 35 cm • **Spread:** to 40 cm

The first time I smelled heliotrope was in Vienna when I stumbled into the
middle of a formal garden and was stopped in my tracks by an intoxicating
vanilla scent all around me. I was surrounded by heliotrope and felt like I
could stand there forever, and now every time I walk by heliotrope I take a
moment and remember that Austrian afternoon.

**The Basics:** Gardeners have been growing heliotrope for years in the house and the garden. It's an average performer and a bit finicky, but its fragrance makes it worth trying. Although heliotrope is a sun lover, it's from Peru where the sun's intensity is tempered by very high humidity. In dry regions of Canada, protect it from afternoon summer sun. If you're planting it in the ground, wait until a week or two after the last frost to make sure the soil has warmed slightly.

It spreads even more than it grows tall.

**Recommended Varieties:** There are several excellent varieties, most with dark blue or purple flowers and at least one white variety. Usually you'll find them in smaller pots, though they're occasionally sold in a standard patio tree form. Before you buy, make sure your plant has rich green leaves that aren't burnt or dried out and that it's well branched. Although its dark foliage is attractive, in spring I see very few people buy them unless they are in bloom.

**Best Uses:** I always recommend keeping heliotrope close to you on the patio, deck or windowsill. Try pairing it with other tropical sun lovers such as ageratum (harmonious colours) or diascia (contrasting colours) in a small, tabletop container. If you're having a picnic, heliotrope makes a novel table centrepiece. Plant it with some chocolate cosmos and lobularia for a delicious way to awaken your taste buds and wow your fellow picnickers.

**Things to Know:** Don't let heliotrope dry out, especially while it is blooming, or the flowers will burn. Butterflies, bees and other pollinators love heliotrope, but it also tends to attract aphids.

Heliotrope brings a cottage feel to containers.

# Impatiens—Double

Botanical Name: *Impatiens walleriana*
Aliases: rose impatiens, busy Lizzie

**Height:** 25–40 cm • **Spread:** 25–40 cm

Native to much of the southern hemisphere, impatiens have become one of the most popular bedding plants in North America because they're garden workhorses and the most reliable performers for shady spots. The rosette flowers on double impatiens are a delicate delight and mound into miniature rose gardens. Mothers love them, and on their day in May a parade of dads with little ones in tow comes through our doors asking for them.

**The Basics:** Double impatiens need to be consistently moist. While they can't be allowed to dry out, they also need well-drained soil so they aren't sitting in water. If they dry out and wilt, they will abort many of their flowers and buds, but more will appear. Morning sun is best (the east side of the house), but an open northern exposure or a shaded or dappled south with be fine. If they become leggy with few flowers, it's a sign that they aren't getting enough sun.

Double impatiens baskets lined up in the back greenhouses before Mother's Day.

Doubles are self-cleaning in that when the blooms expire they will usually simply fall away, but you can help them along with a gentle tussle. Although they are much more compact than they used to be, gently pinching them will encourage them to branch and bloom more and longer.

**Recommended Varieties:** Double impatiens are one of those annuals where it's more helpful to look at the plant itself than to think about what variety it is, as most of the varieties that you find will be excellent. When you're buying, inspect the plants to make sure that they have a compact habit and have a lot of buds (I usually go for buds over flowers). If it doesn't have buds or flowers, it may have been either dried out or recently cut back. Look carefully and you'll be able to see if the leaves, flowers and stems seem a bit too large for the plant (like big feet on a puppy).

Some breeding companies make different varieties according to the size

of the container the impatiens are going in. For example, **'Fiesta'** (40 cm by 40 cm) is best for a larger container (more than 30 cm across), while **'Fiesta Ole'** (25 cm by 25 cm) is best for smaller pots.

**Best Uses:** Double impatiens detest cold soil, so I recommend them exclusively as a container plant, and because they usually form such a pleasing bell-shape I often suggest that they are planted alone. My mom hangs a basket of doubles on a large branch of her shade tree that overhangs the deck. The tree's leaves provide the flowers with dappled sunlight and protection from the wind, and the flowers love it and look like a bouquet of spray roses in a basket all summer long.

**Things to Know:** Double impatiens flowers are beautiful but delicate, and as one good shake of a basket of them will tell you, they aren't the best choice for windy spots.

# Impatiens—New Guinea

**Botanical Name:** *Impatiens* x *hawkeri*
Aliases: busy Lizzie

**Height:** to 30 cm • **Spread:** to 35 cm

Native (of course) to New Guinea, New Guinea impatiens were introduced to North American gardens about 40 years ago but have only recently become compact and colourful enough to be popular for container gardening. They are often the staple filler plant for any tropical-themed container and usually steal the show with colours so warm the big, broad flowers almost shimmer.

**The Basics:** New Guineas are sensitive about water, and if you let them wilt they'll drop their buds. They like slightly more sun than doubles and bloom best with a strong eastern or sheltered southern exposure. Pinch them back if they get leggy, which will happen quicker if they don't have enough sun.

The colours are brilliant in the shade.

**Recommended Varieties:** Pay more attention to the plant than to the name on the tag. Make sure your plant is full and healthy with strong stems and green leaves. If it doesn't have any buds and/or the leaves are browning, it may have dried out and may take a while to bloom. Some varieties boast rich bronze or variegated foliage, though the variegated varieties tend to bloom less.

Think about what size of container you are putting the New Guinea impatiens into when you buy them. The **Celebration Series** (30 cm by 30 cm) works well for larger containers and baskets, while the **Celebrette Series** (25 cm by 25 cm) works well in small to medium containers.

**Best Uses:** Pair New Guineas with shade-loving tropical foliage such as ferns, rex begonias or alocasia. Their lush, rainforest colours and glossy leaves can transform a patio into a tropical oasis. For more colour, blend them with trailing fuchsia, torenia or lobelia. New Guineas also boast enough colour and have a pleasing enough shape to excel on their own, though because they don't trail we usually pair them with a very low vine like creeping Jenny, something without a lot of volume so it won't compete with the impatiens and ruin their crisp bell shape. They're also the best choice for a hanging basket in a shady spot that's also windy.

New Guinea impatiens are a favourite plant for mass plantings across coastal areas of the U.S., but I recommend that they be planted in the ground only in warmer regions of Canada where the soil is warmest and the air is humid.

**Things to Know:** New Guineas, even more so than other impatiens, tend to be stunted by cold Canadian nights, so I don't recommend planting them outside until 2 to 3 weeks after the last frost. Let the garden centres grow them for you until then.

Masses of New Guinea impatiens are beautiful on their own or as fillers.

# Laurentia

Botanical Name: *Laurentia axilleras*
Aliases: star flower, blue star creeper, isotoma

**Height:** to 40 cm • **Spread:** to 40 cm

Laurentia is an Australian native that not many Canadian gardeners know about even though it performs beautifully. Not only is it a colour of blue that is hard to find, but once it starts blooming (it takes a little longer than most to begin) it outshines many things in the garden and requires almost zero maintenance to do so.

**The Basics:** Laurentia likes full sun, but it isn't quite as drought tolerant as some other Aussies and needs to be watered once the soil surface has dried slightly. It has a delicate, airy look to the foliage and the deeply serrated flowers, which look like a child has cut them from folded blue paper. It will be one of the last annuals to bloom but will keep blooming in whatever heat the summer can throw at it, even when the others are spent.

**Recommended Varieties:**
**'Starshine Blue'** has a nice shape, growing into an airy mass of blue and lavender. It is also a very early-blooming variety, whereas others might take until mid-summer before blooming.

**Best Uses:** You can plant laurentia in containers or in the ground. If it's going in the ground I recommend waiting until the soil has warmed up. If in a hanging basket, give it ample room to grow and it will form a globe of gentle blue. Its airy habit, fern-like foliage and soft blue flowers give it a delicate, classic feel that blends well with others like it; I recommend container-mates that can compete with it in aggression and grace, such as 'Peter's Gold Carpet' bidens.

**Things to Know:** Laurentia is not known for anything awful; watch for the usual suspects like aphids. It has been known to cause skin irritation in some people, so wear gloves if you have sensitive skin.

It has an airy, ferny habit and likes being planted alone.

# Osteospermum

Botanical Name: *Osteospermum ecklonis*
Aliases: dimorphotheca, African daisy, cape daisy, blue-eyed
   daisy, star of the veldt

**Height:** to 40 cm • **Spread:** to 50 cm

In their native South Africa, osteospermums—osteos for short—cover whole hillsides with tides of yellow and orange. Osteos are a hit in Canadian yards due both to their love of our cool spring weather and to the masses of colour they paint across our gardens. They've quickly become a container gardening staple, with new varieties being introduced all the time.

**The Basics:** Osteos love cool weather and will tire quickly once the thermometer crosses about 28° C. When this happens, the best thing for them is a haircut and some fertilizer and to wait for the heat to pass. They like to be planted in well-drained soil, and lots of sun will keep them from stretching. Fertilize your osteos regularly to keep them at their best.

**Recommended Varieties:** My personal favourite is the very dwarf **Soprano Series**. They explode with blue and purple flowers and are perfect companions for contrasting plants. The **Symphony Series** has a warm, Mediterranean colour palette of orange, yellow, peach and mango. I love Symphony because it's made for looking great and contrasting in containers. The centre of every flower has a sublimely ultraviolet eye that looks spectacular. **'Voltage Yellow'** is a large, yellow osteo that promises to bloom longer than any other variety.

**Best Uses:** The versatility of osteos makes them an essential annual, and their bright explosions of colour provide instant focal points wherever they are. I love pairing osteos with million bells because both plants love container gardens. Osteos also pair well with other spring lovers such as nemesia. The **spooned** osteos, which have an odd, alien appearance, are excellent both for conversation-starting small containers and for breathtaking mass plantings. You can also take advantge

This 'Asti Purple' took its time blooming but put on a big show when it did.

Although they start out compact, osteos grow quite large and you'll need to trim them if you want them to stay compact.

Symphonies have slightly different habits, which are noticeable if you compare them.

I never get tired of looking at 'Nuanza Copper.'

of spooned osteos' intriguing shape in an architectural planter.

The Soprano Series, with its mushrooming blooms of blues and purples, goes beautifully with million bells, bidens or 'Diamond Frost' euphorbia. With the Symphony Series I usually take advantage of its burgundy-eyed flowers and plant it with pretty much anything with burgundy or wine foliage, such as oxalis, a dark sweet potato vine or 'Plum Superbells' million bells.

The spooned osteos are like having an alien in the yard!

Sopranos are the most compact and bloom like mad!

**Things to Know:** Remember to deadhead osteos once the flowers have wilted; otherwise it will take longer for new buds to form. They tend to get leggy over time, so don't be afraid to trim them back. New, fuller growth will come back in no time.

Although osteos like to dry slightly between waterings, if allowed to go bone dry they may go into dormancy and abort any developing buds.

# Pansy

**Botanical Name:** *Viola* x *wittrockiana*
Aliases: viola, violet (also see below)

**Height:** to 20 cm • **Spread:** to 20 cm

I've never had a day bad enough that looking at a pansy didn't make me feel a little better! Love-in-idleness, the humble flower that Puck dripped into Titania's ear in *A Midsummer Night's Dream*, has been one of the most beloved flowers in the world for centuries. Native to Europe, the original pansy tricolours of the Middle Ages have been hybridized into a never-ending array of sizes, colours and even textures, so that today pansies are one of the most popular plants in Canadian gardens, with new varieties being introduced all the time.

**The Basics:** Pansies are woodland flowers, and their ideal environment is dappled, partial sun. In humid regions they will be able to handle a little direct afternoon sun, but morning sun is ideal. Pansies prefer to dry slightly between waterings.

Pansies prefer cool weather and bloom like crazy in spring and autumn. Through the summer heat you'll see them start to wilt and tire. Don't fight this; the best thing to do is to give them a haircut, keep fertilizing, and enjoy the heat lovers in the garden until the weather cools off. In autumn, when your pansies are blooming again and are nice and full, you'll be glad you cut them back.

## Recommended Varieties:

There are many, many varieties of pansies available, with a multitude of different-sized flowers to choose from in a baffling array of colours. Keep an open mind—usually whenever one catches your fancy, you'll find yourself in love with another one moments later! My personal favourites are the **Citrus Mix** and the **ruffled** pansies, though it's still hard to beat the classic colour of a yellow pansy with a smiling face.

**Violas** have the smallest blooms available, ranging from dime-sized flowers to quarter-sized. They bloom first but tend to get leggy faster than other types. I prefer violas in small containers where I can match them with other cool-weather favourites such as lobularia and nemesia, and where it's easy to give them a haircut when necessary.

The widest selection is in the mid-size flowers. The two largest groups are the **Pure Color Mix**, which bloom in circles of colours as pure and bright as a paint set, and the **blotched** pansies with the smiling faces staring back at you. Don't be shy to try something new, like a pansy with whiskers or a sassy ruffled pansy. With these cheerful little plants, you'll always win!

For large flowers, the **Atlas Series** is a recent addition that comes in two palettes, **'Raspberry'** and **'Blueberry,'** both of which are a lot of fun. **'Majestic Giants'** is still the most asked for large-flowering pansy, but the **Mammoth Series** is just as good or better.

In warmer regions of Canada, watch for hardy **'Icicle'** pansies, which are planted in autumn to bloom early in spring. In colder areas, including the Prairies, plant pansies in spring with the rest of the annuals.

Pansies have the unique gift of being able to make the simplest container instantly beautiful.

Late April is my favourite time at Salisbury because the violas are blooming, and I have them all to myself before the crowds arrive.

**Best Uses:** Pansies are so versatile that the sky is the limit! They work well planted in the ground or in mixed containers, but if you try the latter, don't plant them with anything too aggressive. Wherever they go, their unique aura of cottage gardens, woodland serenity and playful childhood goes with them. No garden should be without at least one.

**Things to Know:** If it's an exceptionally cool and damp year, keep an eye out for powdery mildew.

**What's in a Name:** Being native to Europe, pansies have accumulated a fascinating history of folklore and myth over the past 1000 years (or so). Along with the folkloric tales, most of which involve infatuation, have come a long list of names that the humble violet has been called. Here is a list that I'm sure is not complete:

- bird's eye
- blue violet
- bullweed
- call-me-to-you

Ruffled pansies, like 'Frizzle,' are becoming very popular.

- cuddle me
- English violet
- godfathers
- godmothers
- heart's ease
- Jack-jump-up-and-kiss-me
- Johnny-jump-up
- kiss-her-in-the-buttery
- kiss-me-at-the-garden-gate
- kiss-me-quick
- kit-run-in-the-fields
- love idol
- love-in-idleness
- meet-me-in-the-entry
- pink-eyed John
- pink-of-my-Joan
- sweet-scented violet
- three-faces-under-a-hood
- wild pansy.

Yellow and blue pansies make one of the happiest window boxes imaginable.

# Pentas

Botanical Name: *Pentas lanceolata*
Aliases: star flower, Egyptian star cluster

**Height:** to 40 cm • **Spread:** to 45 cm

Pentas in full bloom, with their radiant flower clusters of five-petalled stars, will light up a container garden like few other plants can. They're not blooming in May when most gardeners are shopping, so they often get passed over for the more colourful nemesias or pansies, but once they open up in the summer heat, few flowers can match their blood red intensity.

**The Basics:** Originally from the Arabian Peninsula, pentas are heat lovers that are mildly drought tolerant and soak up as much sun as possible. In Canada, where we typically plant our annuals during the cool nights of May, pentas' need for heat has limited their popularity. You can count on them, however, to be at their finest through a heat wave that turns all your other annuals (which were fabulous in May, no doubt) into sad droops. Pentas also love humidity and will perform best in regions like southern Ontario and central BC, with their sweltering summers.

Pentas work well here as a border plant in a raised planter.

**Recommended Varieties:** I find that the bold, original red gives the best performance, though there are cultivars in pink, purple, white and bicoloured that are also impressive.

**Best Uses:** Pentas prefer to be planted in a container where the sun can warm their roots from the side as well as from above. They offer a very tropical look, so try mixing them with other tropical sun lovers such as strobilanthes and talinum for a container with both colour and texture. Better yet, put some pentas in a little clay pot (clay absorbs the heat and will keep the roots very warm) on the bistro table in between your lemonade and your novel on a sunny day and enjoy! If you really want a July knockout with as much colour as humanly possible, blend them with gazanias and lantanas—but keep your sunglasses on.

**Things to Know:** Butterflies love pentas. Try to remove the flower heads when they're finished blooming for a longer blooming season. They will tucker out as the summer cools and are a good annual to replace in early September with fresh fall mums, pansies and other autumn flowers.

Kaleidoscope pentas, seen here, are larger than Graffiti pentas.

# Petunia—Upright

**Botanical Name:** *Petunia* x *hybrida*

**Height:** to 35 cm • **Spread:** to 40 cm

Petunias are one of the most popular annuals in the world because they are one of the most versatile, vigorous and colourful plants around. Ever since petunias were first sent from South America to Paris in 1823, they have been so widely loved and hybridized that now they're available in virtually every colour but black (I'm sure they're working on it, though). You can get them mounding, trailing, bicoloured, ruffled, mini, massive, double, veined, starred or frosted. There are always new colours coming out, and almost all of them, because they're petunias, are flowering workhorses.

**The Basics:** Petunias love full sun, though they'll take a break in the scorching heat. They aren't drought resistant and need to be kept consistently moist, which is sometimes a challenge if they're stuffed into a small container. Petunias don't like much humidity and tend to perform best in drier areas of the country, particularly the Prairies.

Petunias respond very well to pinching, so don't be afraid to nip off stems that break away and stretch. They will branch out fuller and bloom more because of it. Although you'll hear many claims about "self-cleaning" petunias, good ol' deadheading will still give you more blooms in the long run.

## Recommended Varieties:

Don't worry as much about what series you are buying as whether the plant is healthy. If a petunia is healthy, it will impress you in the garden and that's all there is to it. That being said, **'Madness'** is the most prolific bloomer that I've ever seen. It's a show-off, performing like crazy whether in mass plantings in a flower bed or in a container garden on the patio. If you're planting in an area very exposed to wind and weather, the **Storm Series** has good weather resistance and the flowers are slightly larger than 'Madness,' though there aren't as many. If you want a bicolour, I love the **Frost Series**, with their cheeky white-rimmed blooms. The doubles are popular and have impressive flowers, but they don't bloom as much as the

Petunias make an excellent, low-cost border.

Nothing says Canada Day like 'Red Frost' petunias.

'Debonair Dusty Rose' is new for 2010.

singles. If you like the really small-flowering petunias, or "millifloras," the new **Picobella Series** is an improvement over the older **Fantasy Series**, bursting into baseballs of blues, pinks and reds.

**Best Uses:** Petunias are one of the most versatile plants in the garden and can be used for pretty much anything. They are an affordable way to fill a border, a flower bed or a large, open space in the garden with colour. You can use them in container gardens as well, but if you use upright petunias in a container, try to match

'Sugar Daddy' is as old-fashioned as they get but is still one of the most asked for varieties.

White is becoming increasingly popular in gardening, and when petunias are white, they are gleaming white.

them with other low aggression annuals such as marigolds and pansies. Try millifloras with French marigolds and violas for a simple, low cost, high impact container.

**Things to Know:** Petunias are very prone to aphids at the end of summer and into autumn. You can fight them if you want, but though I consider petunias to be an excellent spring/summer annual, I find them raggedy in autumn and usually replace them with lovely pansies or mums.

# Schizanthus

**Botanical Name:** *Schizanthus* x *wisetonensis*
Aliases: poor man's orchid, butterfly flower, fringe flower

---

**Height:** to 35 cm • **Spread:** to 25 cm

This Chilean native is a striking plant that has been a fixture of gardening for over a hundred years. In the last several years, however, new introductions have made it a vigorous player in the container gardening craze. In spring it bursts into rounded bloom clusters that look like a swarm of exotic butterflies completely covering the plant.

**The Basics:** Schizanthus prefers consistently moist soil and may need some protection from the afternoon sun. When you water it, try not to water the flowers or leaves. The best way is with a long-neck watering can to the base of the plant. When your schizanthus tuckers out in summer, pinch the main stem and fertilize it, and it may send up a new flush in the cool days of autumn.

'Star Parade' is an old-fashioned variety that is beautiful, though a bit unreliable.

## Recommended Varieties:

Until recently, the schizanthus available was beautiful but inconsistent. New varieties are easily to keep and hold their colour a little longer. I recommend **'Treasure Trove'** (20–25 cm tall). Take a good look at it before you purchase it, and if it's weak, waterlogged or faded, move on. Make sure your plant is well branched or it won't bush out and will look rather silly.

**Best Uses:** Schizanthus looks best in spring before the weather gets too hot, and as such it will probably be one of the prettiest flowers in the garden centre. After a few sensational weeks, however, it will be finished blooming, possibly for the year. Try matching it with other cool-weather beauties, such as nemesia (the fragrance is an extra bonus here) and maybe some juncus for architectural contrast, and put it where you will see it close up. I always keep schizanthus in a small pot close to where I sit in spring so I can enjoy the flowers. After that pot expires, I switch it with a small pot full of pentas and succulents.

If you study its flowers, you'll understand why it's called poor man's orchid. Cut schizanthus flowers will last up to a week and look great, but most people prefer to enjoy them on the patio.

**Things to Know:** Schizanthus doesn't like to dry out and is sensitive to the hot sun.

New varieties of schizanthus can hold their own in the high-performance world of container annuals.

# Strawflower

**Botanical Name:** *Helichrysum bracteatum*
Aliases: everlasting flower, bracteantha, golden everlasting,
    paper daisy

**Height:** to 40 cm · **Spread:** to 35 cm

Like all Aussie plants, strawflower brings a style all its own to the garden. It gets its name from its tactile flowers that feel and crackle like dried straw. Strawflower is a traditional cut flower favourite, and compact varieties bred for container gardening are becoming very popular.

**The Basics:** Strawflowers come originally from the scrublands of Australia and need to be planted in well-drained soil so their feet aren't wet. They tolerate alkaline or slightly chalky soil and thrive most in areas with low humidity. Established plants can take some drought, but keeping the soil slightly moist will keep strawflowers at their best. They are heat tolerant, so don't be afraid to put them in the burning sun. If the flowers go to seed the plant will often take a blooming break, so nip them off before they do.

**Recommended Varieties:** **'Wallaby'** (up to 40 cm tall) is a big plant that will really fill out a container. It blooms like crazy, and you can extend its blooming time by deadheading. **'Sundaze'** (up to 30 cm tall) is smaller but packs a big colour punch. Choose plants that are stocky, well branched and full.

**Best Uses:** Strawflower is perfect for a sunny container garden. I like themed containers, so I would mix it with other Aussies such as flambe and eucalyptus. You can also mix it with other sun lovers such as million bells or verbena. 'Wallaby' is large enough to use as a centrepiece in a small container. 'Sundaze' is a perfect filler plant.

The flowers are excellent for dried arrangements. To use them indoors, cut the flowers before they're fully open (they will open more once cut) and hang them upside down in a dark, well-circulated place to dry.

'Wallaby' comes in a range of fiery colours.

They should last forever when prepared this way.

**Things to Know:** Strawflowers are not as drought tolerant as their name suggests and wilt quickly when they want water. The good news is that they wilt so quickly that you can safely water them before any damage is done.

'Wallaby' looks great in this container with a canna lily.

# Alternanthera

Botanical Name: *Alternanthera dentata*
Aliases: ruby leaf, joy weed, copper leaf, blood leaf, Joseph's coat

**Height:** to 70 cm • **Spread:** to 70 cm

Native to the marshlands of the West Indies, alternanthera has recently made its way to Canadian garden centre shelves, and it's making a big splash. This big, beefy heat lover is part of a group of dark-leaved foliage introductions of the past few years, and it's perfect for contrast and pizzazz in containers.

**The Basics:** Give alternanthera a lot of sun because its colour becomes richer and darker the more sunlight it gets. It needs to be kept consistently moist (many of the species are water plants), though it shouldn't be left in stagnant water. If you feel inclined, it appreciates some cedar mulch, which both keeps moisture in and adds organic matter to the soil (it likes soil as rich and organic as possible). Alternanthera grows quickly in the heat, so it doesn't have a very compact habit.

**Recommended Varieties:**
**'Purple Knight'** (to 70 cm tall and 70 cm wide) is the darkest alternanthera and is my personal favourite. It grows into a thick mound of deep purple. **'Partytime'** (to 60 cm tall and 45 cm wide) is a zesty bicolour of lime green leaves with hot pink on the undersides; the more sunlight it gets, the hotter the colour gets. Another bicolour to watch for is **'Crème de menthe'** (to 60 cm tall and 45 cm wide), which is a vivacious blend of lime green with streaks of cream. **'Royal Tapestry'** (to 35 cm tall and 60 cm wide) is a creeping, copper plant that is great for a ground cover.

**Best Uses:** This is a big foliage annual that grows fast and broad, which makes it perfect for large borders or for big areas you need to fill. Alternanthera's complete lack of subtlety makes it the best for mass plantings. It also looks good in big containers with other big plants such as trailing petunias, bacopa or New Guinea impatiens, with bananas or canna lilies as centrepieces. 'Purple Knight' is excellent for a black theme, or put it in a planter with a black alocasia centrepiece and stark white dahlias and white osteospermums for a shockingly stark contrast. For the bicolours, try pairing 'Partytime' with pink million bells or cobbity daisies. Plant 'Crème de menthe' with cream or white annuals such as bacopa or white nemesia.

**Things to Know:** Alternanthera isn't known for any specific problems or pests. In dry regions watch for the tell-tale webbing that indicates spider mites, which you can help avoid by occasionally hosing down the foliage.

'Royal Tapestry' is a creeper that will really fill out.

# Baby Tears

**Botanical Name:** *Soleirolia soleirolii*
**Aliases:** helxine, mind-your-own-business, angel's tears, peace-in-the-home, Pollyanna vine, mother of thousands, Corsican curse, Irish moss

---

**Height:** to 10 cm • **Spread:** to 35 cm

Baby tears is delicate plant with soft and lusciously tactile foliage that's perfect for aquariums, terrariums and containers in shady nooks. In the last few years gardeners have rediscovered it, and now it's popping up in truly innovative containers, often alongside ferns, which are enjoying their own renaissance. Let your imagination run wild with this gem that is the epitome of "dainty."

**The Basics:** Baby tears needs to be sheltered from direct sun and hot winds. It needs to be kept moist but not soggy and shouldn't sit in water. Try to water it either from the bottom or with a fine spray. If you pour a stream of water on top of it, the battered foliage will die off and leave a brown spot.

**Recommended Varieties:** There are golden and variegated varieties, but they are quite rare. You can also easily propagate baby tears from cuttings if you have a green thumb, some very moist medium and a mister bottle.

**Best Uses:** Usually we think of annuals as beefy, vigorous plants fighting for space in a container. This is a whole different kind of annual gardening, one about attention to small details and a love of lush green jewels. Given the right conditions, baby tears will form a deliciously delicate mat of soft green leaves. Try it in a small container with small ferns or club moss. It is perfect for people who want to create a miniature landscape in an old bird bath or shallow container. Add some small tropical plants, ferns, mosses and large pebbles, and you will have an oasis pretty enough to fuss over.

**Things to Know:** Baby tears is sometimes mistakenly called a *Pilea* or an Irish moss (though it's not a moss), and it is often mixed up with other assorted small tropical plants in the garden centre. Take a picture of it with you because it often isn't marked.

Baby tears is often confused with club moss, shown here. They like the same care.

Baby tears loves humidity, so it's very happy in this Wardian case.

# Begonia—Rex

Botanical Name: *Begonia rex* hybrids
Aliases: painted leaf begonia, beefsteak begonia, king begonia

**Height:** to 30 cm • **Spread:** to 30 cm

Rex begonias have been around for decades as a houseplant but are enjoying a rebirth as a container gardening plant, and justly so! They are a perfect foliage plant for a small to medium container and will tolerate more shade than most foliage. They don't trail, but patterns and textures such as on 'Iron Cross' and 'Escargot' make perfect accents.

Rex begonias will bloom if they have the right conditions.

**The Basics:** The only direct sun that rexes can handle is in early to mid-morning; after that they need to be shaded. They are a bit finicky about moisture and humidity, needing as much humidity as possible (beside a water feature is an ideal spot) while liking their soil to dry slightly between waterings.

**Recommended Varieties:** There are lots of varieties of rex begonia, and the old-fashioned classics often will be lumped in with the new hybrids. One of my favourites is **'Escargot,'** which boasts creeping spirals on its broad leaves. I find that the textured rexes (fuzzy, rippled, etc.) don't grow with quite as much vigour as the others. When you're choosing a plant, make sure it's well branched (more than one or two leaves) and that the soil isn't waterlogged. Check for fuzz on any decaying leaves and avoid them or make sure to clean them off.

**Best Uses:** You can plant rex begonias in the ground or in containers, but if you plant them in the ground make sure they have adequate air circulation around them. In containers they excel as the central feature of a small, lush container, or you can easily blend them into a larger tropical mix with colocasia, fuchsia and coleus. I find that they mix very well with Non-Stop tuberous begonias because both plants like the same moisture levels.

**Things to Know:** As your rex grows, some of the lower leaves will naturally start to wilt and turn brown. Remove these quickly to prevent the onset of a nasty fungus called botrytis, which grows in decaying matter and loves begonias. Removing the leaves also helps with air circulation.

Rex begonias are very happy in the garden, like this 'Escargot.'

# Coleus

**Botanical Name:** *Solenostemon hybrida*
Aliases: flame nettle, painted leaf plant

**Height:** to 50 cm · **Spread:** to 40 cm

Coleus caused quite the craze as a parlour plant in the Victorian era, with new varieties sold at highly inflated prices. It went out of style for much of the 20th century, condemned to obscurity as a houseplant. But with the burst of interest in foliage plants in the 1990s, new varieties began to appear in pots for the garden. Now coleus is a staple foliage container-stuffer; there are hundreds of varieties to choose from, with the colours and textures becoming more intriguing every spring. If you want any upright foliage in your garden, plant coleus first.

**The Basics:** Coleus is a tropical plant, so it doesn't like to dry out and needs some shelter from the afternoon sun. Earlier seed varieties could tolerate only morning sun, but many newer varieties can tolerate a lot of sunlight. Check the tag to know for sure.

Coleus responds well to cutting back and comes back bushier. It will try to bloom in late summer, but do yourself a favour and pinch off the spike as soon as you see it. The flowers aren't worth what the act of blooming does to the shape and performance of the plant.

**Recommended Varieties:** Oh boy! It wasn't long ago that there were only a few banal colours. Now coleus has been bred into every colour you can think of, from soft pastel yellows and siennas to electric blacks and jagged reds. I wouldn't get my heart set on a specific colour; there are so many varieties that most garden centres will carry only a few. Don't worry, you'll find something that you love! Make sure your plant is well branched and has firm stems and rich colours. Pale or faded colours or floppy stems indicate an unhealthy plant.

A big gardener favourite has been **'Kong,'** which is widely available and boasts the largest leaves of any coleus. 'Kong' is great matched with equally large flowers, though I haven't been convinced that it has the best growth habit. You can make 'Kong' bushier by pinching any larger than usual leaves that develop

If you want rich siennas, umbers and rusts in your colour scheme, coleus should be a staple for you.

at the top; they shade the base of the plant, and lower leaves can't grow. Other than 'Kong,' there is a coleus for every mood and design, from the cottage look (traditional oranges and ochres) to the avant-garde (blacks and textured leaves). **'Wizard'** is an old-fashioned shade lover that is good value for mass plantings.

Coleus blends well with garden accessories, such as these ceramic mushrooms.

This speckled coleus adds the perfect touch along with asparagus fern and 'Diva' fuchsia.

The old-fashioned 'Wizard' is small and can be finicky about watering, but it's still the most affordable coleus.

**Best Uses:** 'Kong' looks great in large containers, especially when the flowers on other plants in the container are proportionate to the big coleus foliage (good choices are dahlias and Non-Stop tuberous begonias). Sun-tolerant varieties are good pretty much anywhere. They blend well in any type of container, from a traditional cottage look to exotic foliage planters. Most of them will grow quite large and be impressive plants by mid-summer.

Coleus can be more than just colourful foliage; certain varieties bring a crisp sense of architecture to containers.

Deep red coleus goes brilliantly with New Guinea impatiens.

**Things to Know:** Traditionally many people have brought coleus in during winter for a houseplant, and while it's still possible, the new cultivars are bred for a one-season sprint and get leggy and tired if their lifespan is extended past that. You can take cuttings fairly easily from old plants in early spring; the young plants will perform better than their woody ancestors.

# Croton

**Botanical Name:** *Codiaeum variegatum pictum*
Aliases: rushfoil, garden croton

**Height:** to 80 cm • **Spread:** to 50 cm

Crotons originate in Southeast Asia and the Pacific region. I found them throughout Vietnam forming hedges 2 m tall in the sparse Mekong Delta jungle. This is a classic houseplant that is just beginning to be recognized for its container gardening potential. It boasts a fiery array of yellows, oranges and reds on broad leaves that can be veined, splotched, spotted, curled or twisted.

**The Basics:** Crotons love heat, but without enough humidity our parching afternoon sun will burn them, so keep them sheltered in the afternoon and/or hose down their foliage. They need to stay moist at all times in well-drained soil; some cedar mulch helps. You may find small spikes of pretty but unremarkable white flowers in early summer.

Bring crotons inside over winter, but remember that as they grow taller they will naturally lose leaves on their lower stems (like many tropical plants). Put them back outside in spring when the nights are consistently above 5–8° C.

**Recommended Varieties:** Of the dozens of varieties, **'Petra'** is the most common and easiest to find. It's a gorgeous plant and performs the best, but it's worth checking with larger garden centres for other varieties. There is a huge range of colours and textures. I've counted over 30 cultivars in Florida, but many are hard to get and have poor growth habits. Look for a well-branched, full plant. Sparse crotons haven't had proper care and have dried out.

**Best Uses:** Crotons bring a lot of colour to the table. Try pot-dropping them in a big, tropical container with New Guinea impatiens, sweet potato vine, alocasia, banana and other lush, leafy fare. Whether as a centrepiece in a medium pot or as a filler plant in a large spectacle of a container, they are sure to impress. One of the best uses I've seen is of crotons clustered under an arching brugmansia tree.

Crotons other than 'Petra' are often hard to find.

**Things to Know:** If your croton is in full sun and you notice burning, shelter it right away. Give it a soapy bath if you are bringing it back inside for winter, as it often collects stowaways.

Crotons look great in a fall container as long as they aren't left out in the cold.

# Eucalyptus

**Botanical Name:** *Eucalyptus gunnii*
Aliases: silver drop, cider gum

**Height:** to 75 cm • **Spread:** to 30 cm

Silver drop eucalyptus is from Tasmania and is one of the most suitable eucalyptus for growing in the garden. It's instantly recognizable, with its long stems ringed with silver-blue discs arcing upward from the container. The deliciously subtle colour and crisp architecture make this plant ideal for contemporary themes. Silver drop is also a popular cut flower and lasts a long time in the home.

**The Basics:** Like most annuals from Down Under, eucalyptus tolerates drought and loves the summer heat. It will tolerate sandy soil and isn't a heavy feeder; a monthly shot of fertilizer is fine. If it does flower, you'll be forgiven for not noticing because the blooms aren't very eye-catching. The stems, with their crisp architectural discs and shimmering colour, are all this plant needs to be a hit. You can bring it indoors in autumn (it's actually a tree) and keep it as a tropical plant, though it should continue to live outside in warm weather.

**Recommended Varieties:**
**Silver drop** in a pot (easy to find as a cut) may be hard to track down in Canada; larger garden centres are your best bet for finding it.

**Best Uses:** The best container-mates for eucalyptus are other heat-loving, drought-tolerant annuals. Eucalyptus will thrive in a mixed succulent and/or cactus container. Throw in some flowering kalanchoe or a crown of thorns, and you will have a dramatic container with both architecture and bright colour. For a more classic look, plant it with other annuals that appreciate moderately dry conditions, such as portulaca, gazania or million bells. Silver drop also provides a nice centrepiece contrast with the vertical, burgundy blades of a cordyline. If you're feeling experimental, you can blend eucalyptus with 'Flapjack' kalanchoe and dichondra for a mono-coloured, mono-textured container. Eucalyptus

The rounded leaves alter the whole architecture of this gorgeous succulent planter.

won't perform as well planted in the ground unless the soil is very well drained and preferably elevated.

**Things to Know:** Wait until the coolest spring nights have passed to plant eucalyptus; a wet and cold plant may develop fungus. It isn't particularly susceptible to any pests (in Canada, anyway). Parts of the plant are toxic if eaten.

# Ferns

Botanical Name: see Recommended Varieties

**Height:** to 40 cm • **Spread:** to 50 cm

Ferns have been beloved as houseplants for centuries, but until recently they have only rarely ventured into Canadian gardens. That's changing quickly as magazines and articles everywhere are trumpeting the many virtues of ferns, from their air cleaning prowess to their prehistoric shapes and textures. As a long-time fern lover, I find it a pleasure to watch this rediscovery unfold!

**The Basics:** Although often considered hard to grow (especially the dainty types), I find that ferns are easier to grow outside than inside. They love a medium that's rich in peat (slightly acidic). Make sure to keep them consistently moist; drying ferns out until they shrivel causes long term damage. When you water them make sure to give the fronds a gentle shower. They need to be sheltered from the afternoon sun in all regions and even from the morning sun during dry Prairie summers. Ferns have always thrived in heavily dappled, moist woodland settings. If you have a spot where moss grows on the rocks or from between the stones, it's perfect for ferns.

Ferns will always alter the feel of containers, like this simple recipe with torenia and a frog.

This fern dominates its container!

## Recommended Varieties:

There are many different types of ferns. Some are big show-stoppers, and some are miniature and dainty. With all ferns, make sure you're getting a healthy plant. Inspect your fern before you buy it. If it has curled or crispy leaves then it has probably been dried out (very common, especially in the box stores) and will take a long time to rebound. Here are some of the most popular types that are best suited for container gardening:

**Asparagus ferns** (*Asparagus densiflorus*) are the most commonly used ferns in container gardening. They are big-volume plants that grow in long spires that flop down from the container. In the home, they will make a mess if allowed to dry out. **'Foxtail'** produces much more compact spires but is often hard to find and expensive.

This Boston looks perfect with a simple lobelia.

Asparagus ferns are very common in container gardening.

**Bostons** (*Nephrolepis exalta*) are ubiquitous houseplants that are also excellent air cleaners; they will remove harmful chemicals and even bacteria from the air in your home. Air cleaning plants are especially great for people with allergies or homes containing older building materials. There are many cultivars, and often the differences are so subtle that it takes a botanist to tell them apart. A quirky exception is **'Fluffy Ruffle,'** a vivacious fern that should not be planted by anyone who takes their containers too seriously.

**Maidenhairs** (*Adiantum* spp.) are my personal favourites. They are the most delicate ferns, with fronds like fine woven lace and gently arching habits. They need the most protection from the sun and require the most humidity; they are a favourite terrarium plant.

**Painted ferns** (*Athyrium* spp.) are larger than many of the others. Their fronds turn rich coppers and umbers, often in autumn, and they are commonly seen in perennial beds. **Japanese painted ferns** are a crisp silver colour. There are many types, so check the size before you buy to make sure that it will fit into your design.

**Plumosa** (*Asparagus plumosus*) is ideal for anyone planning an oriental theme. This small, very delicate fern arcs over its container like an umbrella, sheltering the baby tears underneath. Plumosa is perfect for containers that are dainty, finicky and beautiful.

**Staghorns** (*Platycerium* spp.) are ancient giants making a comeback and are appearing in some of the trendiest new containers. Their statement-making, antler-shaped fronds instantly make their container look lumbering, prehistoric and awesome. I love stags, so it's a treat to see them being used in different ways. They don't need quite as much water as other ferns, and don't worry about the brown fuzz that appears on the ends of the fronds in mid-summer—it is the spores.

Boston ferns and peace lilies are two great air-cleaning plants.

**Best Uses:** Wherever they go, ferns bring their unique sense of woodland solace and peace. They are natural community plants and benefit from being around other plants. Their favourite companions are orchids; the two have evolved together for millennia and share a beneficial gas exchange. A simple orchid and fern mix makes a perfect low maintenance, high impact container. Ferns also thrive planted in the ground in shady nooks of the garden or in rocks around a water feature.

**Things to Know:** Ferns get very few pests, which makes them perfect for bringing inside in autumn.

'Fluffy Ruffle' is the jester of the fern world.

#

Botanical Name: see Recommended Varieties

**Height:** variable • **Spread:** variable

Herbs can do anything! They have been cherished for millennia for their medicinal properties, and Canadian gardeners are now discovering how beautiful they are in container gardening. Often overlooked as ornamentals because they lack showy flowers, what they offer is much better: gorgeous colours and textures that get healthier the more you pick them. Although they are far from new, their rapid growth in popularity and the changing ways in which people are using them has made them indispensible for this book.

**The Basics:** There are hundreds of different herbs so care instructions will vary sometimes, but for the most part here are the simple rules of thumb. They love the sunlight, so plant them in full or partial sun and let the surface dry slightly between waterings. Don't be shy about pinching them back. Every time I pinch my herbs, whether it's for a pizza, a salad or just to graze, they grow back fuller and bushier. They like some fertilizer but aren't picky about what kind.

**Recommended Varieties:** The number of herbs available in the past couple of years has exploded. Below is a very brief list of some of the most popular types. For more on herbs, consult a herb book or look online at one of the many excellent herb sites.

Marigolds are very useful for keeping pests off your herbs.

**Basil** (*Ocimum basilicum*) is very popular. We sell more **sweet** basil than any other herb, not to mention **Thai** basil, **lemon** basil, **cinnamon** basil, **lettuce** basil, **purple** basil, **'Green Globe'** basil and so on. Basil is notoriously hard to keep alive, and those who do manage it are rewarded with an increasingly woody plant with less flavour. Keep basil in its own pot, enjoy it while it's fresh, and replace it when it starts to decline. It likes to dry significantly between waterings.

**Rosemary** (*Rosmarinus officinalis*) is my favourite herb. Many people say keeping a pot of rosemary on your night table is a cure for depression; rub some on your hands and you'll be a believer! **'Tuscan Blue'** is an upright variety with the most full-bodied flavour. There are also trailing varieties as well as novelty types such as **'Barbecue.'** Remember that rosemary is native to the Mediterranean and as such likes a lot of sun and needs to dry between waterings.

**Sage** (*Salvia* spp.) doesn't compete with other leafy annuals in size and lushness, but the olive green, textured cream and subtle purples of the coloured sages make a gorgeous container. Like succulents, they have a beauty all their own.

Basil comes in several colours and many flavours.

Purple sage is a gorgeous container stuffer, thanks to its subtle texture and colour.

**Best Uses:** Basil is the classic summer herb for mixing with salads, white meat or anything with tomato in it (or just a basil and fresh beefsteak tomato sandwich). Rosemary adds a unique, instantly recognizable shape to a container with other heat lovers such as succulents or 'Diamond Frost' euphorbia. I like some sage with meat dishes, especially pork and poultry. Just throw a handful in the pan or the pot, and diffusion will do the rest. Make sure to keep a bit of it for an attractive garnish.

Herbs are tastier when they are young, so graze, graze, graze! At my house, many a good summer

Rosemary can be very effective as a statement plant.

Herbs are very versatile and can be planted in almost anything as long as it has drainage.

barbecue has been made great after a stroll through the garden tearing off bits of sage, rosemary and basil. Their growth habits are versatile enough to go with almost anything. My wife likes to plant them beside some ferny marigolds (*Tagetes* spp.), which helps keep the critters away.

**Things to Know:** When you're including edible food in a container, I recommend making sure that everything in the container is edible. Mixing herbs with a plant with toxic leaves (e.g. datura) could lead to some serious unintended problems for people grabbing clumps of leaves.

**Botanical Name:** *Iresine herbstii*
Aliases: beefsteak plant, chicken gizzard

**Height:** 25–90 cm • **Spread:** 30–60 cm

Given the name "beefsteak" because its leaves look like a steak (about medium rare), iresine is a low maintenance Brazilian that is easy to grow and brings potent, contrasting colour into your yard. It can be either a low growing accent plant or a rugged centrepiece, with its blood red veins pulsing drama into your container.

**The Basics:** Iresine is heat tolerant and brash. Some varieties can handle full sun, but many need some protection from the afternoon scorch. Keep the soil a bit moist because iresine doesn't like to dry out; mulch helps.

**Recommended Varieties:** Different varieties of iresine grow to very different sizes. **'Purple Lady'** is a compact variety, rarely growing over 25 cm tall. Its colour is richest in full sun. **'Bloodleaf'** is a compact variety with blood red veins, and it prefers partial sun. **'Blazin Lime'** is a vigorous grower that needs the most sun protection and boasts green leaves with striking cream veins. **'Blazin Rose'** is the largest iresine; its blood-veined leaves can stretch into a small shrub almost 90 cm tall. It needs some afternoon protection.

Iresine is growing in popularity, so most garden centres will have it. Make sure you choose a well-branched plant; a spindly plant won't develop the kind of volume iresine needs to be at its best.

**Best Uses:** Try 'Bloodleaf' in a medium container with some red dianthus or red dahlias for a rich harmony. Throw in some flambe for a provocative combination. Try 'Purple Lady' in a pot with pentas and dichondra, and it will sparkle in the summer heat. It makes an excellent contrast plant in a small to medium container.

'Blazin Lime' anchors this container on an Earl's patio.

The larger varieties are best used as centrepieces in tropical- or foliage-themed containers. Use the Blazin Series in larger pots with tropical colours, like New Guinea impatiens, fuchsia or trailing begonia. Blazin iresines have a sparse enough growth habit that other big-volume plants grow nicely between their branches, creating a dynamic container. Large iresine is also an effective landscaping plant.

**Things to Know:** If your plant gets leggy, nip a bit off the tops of the vines to encourage it to branch out fuller than before. If it gets too crowded, watch for powdery mildew.

'Blazin Rose' can take the full, hot sun of a downtown street.

**Botanical Name:** *Brassica oleracea*
Aliases: flowering cabbage

**Height:** to 30 cm • **Spread:** to 45 cm

Kale is an autumn classic that many gardeners have begun using in spring as a uniquely textured filler. Its dense, compact habit makes it an anchor when placed amongst other annuals, and its ruffled rosettes have such clean, uncluttered symmetry that it's hard not to admire them.

**The Basics:** Kale is easy to grow from seed. It likes sun but not too much heat; heat mutes its colours and promotes flowering, which ruins its shape, but cool temperatures give it a firm shape and really make its colours richer. I suspect that it often saves its richest colours for after the first frost. When you're buying kale, make sure it's not rootbound; rootbound kale often won't grow much more even after it's planted.

**Recommended Varieties:** The variety to look for depends on what shape you want your kale to be. My favourite is the **Pigeon Series** because they have the most compact shape, closely resembling cabbage but with striking colour in the centre. **'Pigeon Victoria'** is a beautiful pink. **'Nagoya'** is almost as compact, with dramatically ruffled leaves that bring a strong dose of texture. **'Peacock'** has a mushrooming, fan-shaped habit.

**Best Uses:** Kale is mostly used in autumn, when the cool nights will make its colours vivid. It is often hardy to -7° C and looks beautiful in containers next to black-eyed Susan and garden mums. 'Peacock' looks lovely in the centre of a small container with pansies planted under and around it. Kale's texture and dense architecture also make it a surprising but fitting match with succulents in a contemporary planter.

It performs even better planted in the ground, where its roots stay

Their stable size makes them adaptable to unique containers, like this wagon.

cooler, and its uniform shape makes it ideal for mass plantings. It will be one of the last annuals alive and, even when it does freeze, it will look great silhouetted against the snow.

**Things to Know:** Watch for the central flower spike starting to emerge in late summer, and snap it off. It will try to bloom if it's in a hot location. Once kale blooms, its shape becomes unpleasantly distorted. Also keep your eye out for green worms that might be munching on it.

Kale matches surprisingly well with succulents.

# Oxalis

**Botanical Name:** *Oxalis regnellii*
Aliases: false shamrock, wood sorrel

**Height:** to 35 cm • **Spread:** to 40 cm

*Oxalis* is a massive genus that is ubiquitous all over the world. Once only for leprechauns, new varieties of oxalis introduced in the past few years have changed how we see this lucky woodland plant forever! It may be closely related to clover, but its colour, versatility and workhorse performance make it an exciting new arrival.

**The Basics:** Oxalis loves the dappled shade of the woods, and as such needs some shelter from the afternoon sun, especially on the dry Prairies. It doesn't like to dry out and will tell you promptly when it's thirsty by flopping down and playing dead, but it also doesn't want to be soggy. Like most high performance annuals, it's been bred to require regular fertilizer.

**Recommended Varieties:** Iron cross (*O. triangularis*) has been a low-key yet beloved houseplant for decades. For an annual, however, I heartily recommend the new **Charmed Series** from Proven Winners, especially the wine colour because I'm a sucker for its foliage. These plants require almost no maintenance to look stunning. The first year I grew the Charmed Series I was surprised at how large the leaves got when I gave the plant enough space. This is no ordinary clover; its leaves are broad palettes of pure, rich colour punctuated by nodding, white trumpet flowers. Its habit gets a bit large and sloppy as it matures, but that just adds to its charm! **'Molten Lava'** is the most compact of the series. I find it an intriguing novelty because of its coppery yellow foliage, but it's a tiny plant that rarely fills out the 10 cm pot we plant it in.

**Best Uses:** Oxalis is perfect in a patio pot or a hanging basket, and although it can be planted on its own and still look great, it has those bewitching burgundy tones that seem made to contrast with other

Put 'Charmed Velvet' with other black plants for a gothic contemporary look.

plants. My favourite use for it is to pair it with Symphony Series osteospermums, with their burgundy flower centres. For a striking monochromatic look, pair it with red canna lilies, 'Red Shield' hibiscus and/or pentas. Reserve 'Molten Lava' for small containers because it will easily be lost in a larger one.

**Things to Know:** Older varieties of oxalis are traditionally houseplants, but though you can bring a Charmed oxalis in for winter, it really hasn't been bred to live longer than one season and will probably not do well through winter.

Although its large size often surprises people, oxalis stays remarkably compact.

# Strobilanthes

**Botanical Name:** *Strobilanthes dyerianus*
Aliases: Persian shield

**Height:** to 65 cm • **Spread:** to 50 cm

Native to Burma (Myanmar), Persian shield is one of the most uniquely coloured annuals in this book; its metallic purple sheen absolutely pops out of a container when it catches the midday sun. It's a tropical heat lover that's easy to grow and is perfect for inspiration and experiments because it goes with almost anything.

**The Basics:** When you're thinking of where put it, think Burma. It wants the hottest, most humid spot it can get. Keep the soil moist because it doesn't like to dry out. Its colour is most vivid in a hot, sun drenched spot; likewise it will fade in a shady spot.

**Recommended Varieties:** **Persian shield** is the only variety right now, but keep an eye out for new introductions. The metallic leaves are so unique that you can be sure breeding companies are working to do more with them.

**Best Uses:** Try putting this plant in a container with any of your favourite heat lovers in as hot a spot as possible. The metallic purple of strobilanthes goes beautifully with many colours. It's perfect for people like me who like to push the limits of contrast! I mix it up with the burning red of pentas, the hot Mediterranean colours of lantana and the hot chartreuse of sweet potato vine for jaw-dropping colour. Its purple highlights also make it a perfect match with scaevola or purple million bells. For a harmonious container, blend strobilanthes with purple fountain grass, black sweet potato vine and purple verbena or million bells. I don't recommend planting it in the ground because it doesn't like cold feet.

**Things to Know:** If you find that it is becoming stringy, you can pinch it to encourage bushiness, but pinch

Make sure your strobilanthes is well branched.

only slightly—the Canadian growing season is short enough without having to wait for your strobilanthes to shine.

It looks great with other cool colours, such as silvers or blues.

# Succulents

Botanical Name: see Recommended Varieties

**Height:** 10–50 cm • **Spread:** 10–30 cm

Once considered only houseplants in Canada, succulents are now some of the trendiest container gardening plants around. It's hard to flip through a gardening magazine these days without finding something about them. They are low maintenance, visually striking and have so much personality that you'll want to name them. Watch for their sophisticated brand of beauty to become a staple in container gardening in the next few years.

**The Basics:** Succulents are a massive group of plants (including cacti) that survive in harsh conditions around the world because of their ability to store moisture in their fleshy leaves. They need a lot of light but may burn if they are suddenly exposed to direct afternoon sun; they will need to be introduced gradually. Plant them in a very well-drained soil (add some gravel or sand to the mix) so that the roots are never sitting in water. That being said, water them generously in summer when they're growing.

## Recommended Varieties:

Although succulents are becoming rapidly more popular as annuals, with many gardeners now asking for different types of them by name, they are still often sold within a big grouping of assorted plants somewhere in the houseplant section in the back of the store. Keep an open mind; if your heart is set on a specific species or variety, you may have trouble finding it. Here are a few of the most popular groups:

**Aeoniums** (*Aeonium* spp.) are very trendy succulents, often with near-black foliage. Designing magazine favourites and widespread through Europe, they are making their way slowly into Canada but can be hard to find. Call around to larger garden centres; they will be worth the hunt. Although ebony aeoniums are the most popular, there are also many varieties of greens, bicolours and even mottled types with irregular lumps on their leaves.

**Aloes** (*Aloe* spp.) come in varieties both traditional and cutting edge. The most popular is **aloe vera**, but watch for **'Retro Gang,'** a mottled aloe from Proven Winners, though it may not be widely available in Canada.

**Echeverias** (*Echeveria* spp.) are rosette succulents that are similar to aeoniums. Their visual appeal comes from the mix of subtle, stunning colour tones and clean architectural lines, all in a delightfully compact plant. As they grow, the rosette remains but a stem develops underneath, pushing it upward.

**Kalanchoes** (*Kalanchoe* spp.) include some of the most bizarre-looking succulents and are my personal favourites. Watch for the furry-leaved **panda plant** (*K. tomentosa*) and the red-tinged, paddle-leaved **'Flapjack'** (*K. thyrsiflora*; paddle plant).

'Flapjack' kalanchoe is one of my favourites.

Assorted succulents add architectural drama to this modern container.

Flowering kalanchoes are very easy to find and add a lot of colour to succulent containers.

**Best Uses:** Far from the glitz and glitter of most annuals, the beauty of succulents is in the interplay of subtle blues and burgundies and in their captivating architecture, which ranges from the mathematical (echeveria) to the quirky (kalanchoe). Architectural plants, with their vividly symmetrical features and crisp lines, are one of the most modern trends in container gardening. For a striking architectural container, match succulents with the stiff burgundy of a cordyline, the contrasting white veins of an alocasia or the silver circles of a eucalyptus. Succulents also look great on their own or with other succulents of different groups. You can buy these mixed

Aeonium in a container from the Oxford Botanical Garden.

Mixed succulent planters have a beauty all their own!

succulent gardens from a garden centre or easily make them yourself.

The unorthodox ways we're using succulents are increasingly challenging the notion of what a container is. They can appear as pizzas, wreaths or even as the containers themselves!

**Things to Know:** Succulents aren't susceptible to many pests. As such, they are perfect to pot-drop, wherein you bring them in for winter and keep them for years. They are small and grow so slowly that in a few years, when you have grown one to specimen size, you'll want to make it a focal point.

# Talinum

Botanical Name: *Talinum paniculatum*
Aliases: fameflower, jewels of Opar

**Height:** to 70 cm • **Spread:** to 35 cm

Talinum is a chartreuse foliage plant that offers more than meets the eye. Gardeners who plant it in spring usually think they will be getting a striking foliage plant and are often surprised to see that the foliage is just the beginning. A few weeks later, tall panicles of dozens of tiny, sparsely set pink flowers leap 45 cm upward to jazz up the container's shape and texture. It's like two plants in one.

**The Basics:** Although it's notoriously invasive in the southern U.S., in Canada talinum is a pleasure to have in a container. In full sun it will grow into a small, bell-shaped shrub about 45 cm tall. Although its foliage gives the impression of a lush tropical plant, it has a reputation for being extremely drought resistant. It's very susceptible to cold nights, so don't plant it until one to two weeks after your more cold-tolerant annuals.

**Recommended Varieties:** **'Limon'** is the chartreuse talinum that has become popular very quickly. It is one of the most impressive new plants in the greenhouse. Watch for **'Verde,'** which is a green-leaved talinum that is slightly larger and promises taller flower panicles.

**Best Uses:** Chartreuse foliage just cries out for contrasting colours, so I like blending talinum in a container with some purple million bells, purple fountain grass or a Soprano Series osteospermum. Talinum sends up tall panicles of dainty, pink flowers in late spring. These panicles provide a pleasant pink swarm that blends well with the crisp lines of cordyline or phormium as they sway in the breeze. The flowers are followed by caramel-coloured seedpods. Talinum's ability to tolerate drought also makes it a good companion for gazania, succulents or eucalyptus.

**Things to Know:** Watch for aphids, especially late in the season when annuals' immune systems weaken.

The cloud-like buds open into tiny, pink flowers before turning into dark red seedpods.

It loves being paired with heat-loving container-mates, like this celosia.

# Bacopa

Botanical Name: *Sutera cordata*
Aliases: water hyssop

**Height:** to 20 cm • **Spread:** to 70 cm

This one changed all the rules! Twenty years ago it was a nondescript swamp weed from southern France that nobody would have guessed could be hybridized into a container gardening phenomenon. Within two years of its arrival, bacopa had every garden centre starting to pay attention and thinking that maybe, just maybe, gardening was changing in a fundamental way. Hats off to bacopa; I make sure to include some in my garden.

**The Basics:** The terminology gets confusing: although the genus *Bacopa* looks a lot like the annual bacopa, the annual bacopa is actually in the genus *Sutera*. 'Bacopa' is actually the brand name given to it by Proven Winners, but it has become so ubiquitously successful that it has become the accepted plant name.

By any name, it's a great garden performer. Fertilize it liberally and keep the soil moist, and it will sparkle with five-petalled stars set against semi-dark foliage in full sun or light shade. Bacopa has a very recognizable, pungent scent; don't rub the leaves if it's not for you.

## Recommended Varieties:
**'Snowflake'** started it all, and, though the other types are improving, it is still the leader of the pack. **'Giant Snowflake'** has the largest flowers of any bacopa I've seen on a healthy, robust plant. **'Abunda'** has excellent heat tolerance.

There are several colours of bacopa available, from pink to purple, and though they are an intriguing novelty plant, I find them to be stringy with few flowers. Look for an improved pink and blue from Proven Winners. **'Gold 'n' Pearls'** has golden leaves with a compact growth habit. There are also some double whites available, though I haven't seen how they perform.

With this little plant everything depends upon how it's grown. The best genetics in the world won't rescue it from the hands of a poor

Look for a well-branched plant so that your bacopa has some volume.

'Gold 'n' Pearls' is smaller, but its charming foliage makes it a nice touch with this baby's breath.

Bacopa blends well with 'Blue-Violet Tapien' verbena both in texture and in habit.

grower. No matter the variety, when you're buying, always look for a plant that is compact and well branched (otherwise you'll end up with one dangling string) and has dark green leaves. If the plant hasn't been fertilized properly, the leaves will be pale green. Stringy, floppy stems are an indication that it has been grown too warm, and stems with no flowers mean that it has dried out.

Blue bacopa started out very stringy but is constantly being improved upon.

**Best Uses:** At the greenhouse we put bacopa in most of the mixed baskets we create. It's an excellent spiller because it doesn't have a lot of volume (so it doesn't compete with the filler plants) and blooms all summer as long as it doesn't dry out. It's also very versatile and fits in with almost any combination, from contemporary to traditional. Bacopa adds visual appeal without stealing the spotlight. It's both a dominant and a neutral presence in a container; it's a big, noticeable plant, but its white, generic flowers go with almost any colour or textural theme.

**Things to Know:** Bacopa needs a lot of water tends to dry to a crisp quickly on a hot day. This doesn't kill the plant—it actually bounces back nicely—but it won't bloom for weeks afterward.

# Begonia—Trailing

**Botanical Name:** *Begonia* x *hybrida*

**Height:** to 50 cm • **Spread:** to 1 m

Old-fashioned trailing begonias have been around a long time as house-plants, but recent introductions of freely blooming, high performance container varieties have Canadian gardeners taking a second look, often with their mouths hanging open! Forming giant balls of colour that spill out of the container in all directions, trailing begonias are now one of the show-stoppers of the modern garden.

**The Basics:** Trailing begonias can tolerate more sun than most begonias can, but I would still protect them from the afternoon sun in dry regions. They are a tropical plant and as such need to be planted in a rich medium (preferably peat moss based) that is also well drained. They love humidity and perform best in the more humid areas of Canada.

**Recommended Varieties:** **Illumination Series** begonias grow to 30 cm tall and spread up to 90 cm. They are eager performers with a lot of volume and scores of pendulous, double flowers. **'Apricot'** is my favourite colour, producing yellow flowers with a hint of orange. **Pin-Up Series** begonias grow to 20 cm tall and spread up to 30 cm. They are smaller plants with single flowers in very warm oranges and reds. **'Dragon's Wing'** grows 35 cm tall and spreads to 45 cm. It performs very well in humid regions and tends to keep a pleasing, mounded habit of glossy leaves punctuated by deep red flowers. **'Million Kisses'** is a new heat- and sun-tolerant variety that is supposed to perform well even in full sun.

There has been a lot of buzz in the gardening world about the introduction of **'Bellagio'** (double flowering) and **'Mandalay'** (single flowering) begonias, which are bred to withstand more heat, humidity and sun than any previous begonias. They were supposed to be available in 2009, but they are delayed and are probably still a couple of years away.

Meanwhile, other introductions are set to steal their thunder!

**Best Uses:** I usually prefer planting trailing begonias in their own hanging basket. They are big plants, and they can look awkward in a small or even mid-sized container with other plants. That being said, Pin-Up begonias are small enough to look good in mixed containers. In a large container with other big, tropical shade lovers (e.g., banana, 'Kong' coleus and hibiscus) where the theme is "big," any begonias will look fabulous.

**Things to Know:** Although powdery mildew tends not to be a major problem with trailing begonias (because they are usually planted above the ground where there is better air circulation), I still recommend drying them out slightly between waterings.

Trailing begonias have a lot of volume and are great for big, beefy containers.

# Bidens

Botanical Name: *Bidens ferulifolia*
Aliases: tickseed, Apache beggartick, fern-leaf beggartick,
    bur-marigold

---

**Height:** to 30 cm • **Spread:** to 70 cm

*Bidens* is a large genus that has become famous for its bright primary yellow flowers and its sticky seeds that love to snag clothing. They are lovely, if aggressive, annuals, and with their lacy foliage and cheerful, starry flowers, they have a refreshing, airy feel to them. They will keep blooming all summer as long as they are in the sun.

**The Basics:** Bidens can handle full sun even in dry regions. It flowers like crazy and, with enough light, should go all summer and into autumn. If it gets leggy, don't be shy about giving it a good trimming; it will grow back before you know it.

**Recommended Varieties:** Different varieties of bidens have radically different growth habits. **'Peter's Gold Carpet'** is the original variety and the most—ahem—out of control. It grows outward quickly and in every direction into a graceful, airy array of bright yellow stars held aloft on stems of feathered foliage. It's stunning, but make sure to give it ample space, and I wouldn't plant it with anything that isn't aggressive. **'Solaire'** is a more recent introduction from Proven Winners that is advertised as being well behaved. That's an understatement, as 'Solaire' is actually more a filler than a trailer, keeping its very, very compact habit as a pleasant, bright yellow clump.

'Solaire' is compact and well behaved.

'Peter's Gold Carpet' and 'Solaire' are two types of dozens, but they represent the two polarized growth habits you'll encounter no matter what variety you choose. When you're at the garden centre, the different growth habits will be obvious. The sprawling types will be leggy and probably tangled with their neighbours. The clumping types will be a tight clump punctuated by a few yellow flowers.

**Best Uses:** Bidens are best in hanging baskets and other containers where they can trail freely.

Choose your bidens depending on the look you're going for. If you want an open, airy feel to your container, choose 'Peter's Gold Carpet' or another variety with a sprawling habit. For a truly graceful, airy container, match this bidens with gaura, euphorbia and phlox. If you like your containers to be a little more "tucked-in," choose a clumping variety like 'Solaire' and mix it with ageratum and nemesia.

**Things to Know:** Keep your eye out for powdery mildew if bidens is crowded and wet. Beneficial insects such as bees and butterflies love bidens, especially the airy varieties of the plant.

# Flambe

**Botanical Name:** *Chrysocephelum apiculatum*
Aliases: Australian daisy, common everlasting, yellow buttons

**Height:** to 35 cm • **Spread:** to 45 cm

Australia has been a gold mine for hot new annuals in the past few years, and flambe is no exception. I debated how to categorize this plant because it is as much a filler as a trailer, and it is grown as much for its foliage as for its flowers; its outside-the-box, hard-to-pigeon-hole nature is why I like it!

**The Basics:** This one performs best in the hottest, driest spot you have. It needs very well-drained soil (it tolerates grit and sand) and is drought tolerant. It prefers dry climates and is perfectly suited to dry Prairie summers.

**Recommended Varieties:** Common everlasting is not a new plant, but **'Flambe'** is the first time it has been hybridized specifically for container use. 'Flambe' is a brand name, and as of this writing it's the only cultivar widely available (I'm sure others are on the way).

**Best Uses:** I recommend flambe for container use only; the cold ground will stunt it. It is perfect for a low maintenance container. Go ahead and put it in the hottest spot you can find—it won't mind—it won't be as hot as Australia! Flambe performs very well as an accent plant; its very sparse habit enables it to intermingle easily with its container-mates, and it has the unique habit of weaving among and blooming between the flowers of other fillers, sprinkling its container-mates with small, yellow spheres and spicing up the flat profiles of million bells with its arcing silver stems. Its silver tinge, subtle yellow flowers and branching habit make it an excellent partner with yellow or yellow/orange bicolour million bells. You could also match it with some purple osteospermums for a contrasting container. It will last a long time as a cut flower, but its rather short, arcing stems will look a bit awkward.

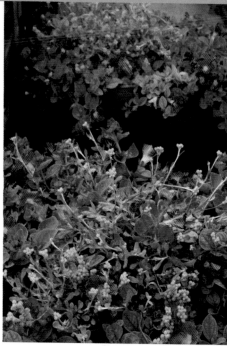

Flambe's sparse growth habit makes it perfect for growing in between other annuals.

**Things to Know:** Flambe doesn't attract pests, so any problems you encounter will probably be from overwatering. Make sure it's never sitting in water and that it has enough air circulation that its foliage dries quickly.

Its upward-arcing habit will make the shape and profile of a planter more interesting.

# Fuchsia

**Botanical Name:** *Fuchsia* spp.
Aliases: lady's earrings

**Height:** 15 cm–1 m • **Spread:** 30 cm–1 m

There are almost 100 species of fuchsia, most of which are native to South and Central America, not to mention the countless hybrids. They have been popular house and garden plants for centuries, and the number of hybrids that have been developed and lost since their introduction to Britain in 1789 dwarfs the number that now exist, though many of the original varieties are still popular. Recently, new varieties of fuchsia that are more free flowering and have a more compact habit than ever before have made Canadian gardeners take renewed notice. I think it's safe to say that fuchsia will never go out of style—it will just keep evolving.

**The Basics:** Fuchsias are iconic shade lovers and prefer morning sun and/or heavily dappled afternoon sun. They like rich, organic soil, so I recommend a peat moss based mix. Keep their soil evenly moist; they can't dry out but don't like wet feet. Many varieties grow quickly into big plants that become very delicate; try to put them in a spot where they have ample room and don't have to be moved.

**Recommended Varieties:** There are two kinds of fuchsia: the old and the new. I'm a sucker for the classics, and in my opinion, you can't beat the rich purple and red of **'Dollar Princess,'** the extra-soft, double blooms of **'Pink Marshmallow'** or the cherry and whipped-cream blossoms of **'Swingtime.'**

Newer varieties are more compact than the classics and are more freely blooming. **'Shadowdancer'** grows only 20–30 cm tall and looks like it has clusters of exotic earrings hanging from it. The variety that only seems to get more popular with time is **'Gartenmeister.'** Besides being one of the best annuals to attract hummingbirds, it also boasts rich red foliage, an excellent growth habit and clusters of vivid red, tubular flowers all summer long.

**Best Uses:** Traditional varieties of fuchsia are used almost exclusively in hanging baskets and containers where they can cascade freely. Newer varieties are more compact and are better suited for mixed containers. I

'Gartenmeister' is a perfect filler for a bulky, lush container with ferns and iresine.

often see 'Gartenmeister' as a tree-form centrepiece in the middle of a large container.

**Things to Know:** Although it can be easily overwintered inside, keep in mind that fuchsia is very attractive to bugs, especially whiteflies, and more often than not your plant will have stowaways that may be very hard to get rid of.

Fuchsia looks great in this moss basket with lobelia.

# Lantana

Botanical Name: *Lantana camara*
Aliases: shrub verbena, Spanish flag, red sage, yellow sage

**Height:** to 40 cm • **Spread:** to 50 cm

Lantana boasts a palette of colours so fiery they look almost like glowing embers spreading across the patio. These luscious colours, along with its easy-growing nature, have given it a recent spike in popularity, and breeders have been scrambling to bring new lantanas to the market. If you have a spot that's too hot for anything else, lantana will thrive there all summer.

**The Basics:** In tropical areas of Africa and in the Middle East, some species of lantana are considered a noxious weed—in Canada that just means that it is a fast-growing annual. Lantana is a vigorous heat lover that will bloom like crazy during a heat wave when the other plants in your yard are sweltering. Warm, humid regions are the best; on the Prairies, cold spring nights will slow it down, so I recommend waiting until the nights have warmed slightly before planting it outside. It is drought tolerant but will still have to be watered and fed regularly, especially when it's hot, to keep it blooming.

**Recommended Varieties:** There are dozens of varieties of lantana, and I hesitate to recommend one over the other. Because they're a summer plant, they probably won't be blooming when you buy them in May. Before you buy, look for a plant with as many branches as possible. The bushier the plant is, the fuller it will be and the more impact it will have when it's flowering. Lantana is also available in a standard form (mini tree) that makes an interesting patio plant. Besides its usual flaming palette, it also comes in white and purple.

**Best Uses:** Lantana is great for containers or hanging baskets in the full, hot sun. Its warm, Mediterranean oranges and yellows pair well with other luscious colours. Try matching it with citrus-coloured gazania for heat-loving harmony or with purple pentas for contrast. You could also try it with scaevola for an intriguing hanging basket combination. Of course, purple fountain grass or millet always looks good. There are landscape varieties bred for ground cover, but they are best in U.S. gardens where the soil is warmer; they don't perform well in the cold Canadian ground. Lantana is one of the best annuals for attracting bees and butterflies.

**Things to Know:** All parts of lantana are poisonous. Watch for whiteflies, which are easy to spot (pure white and heart-shaped). They are fairly easy to eliminate with a high pressure spray across the undersides of the leaves.

'Grape' lantana is a bright, fruity purple.

# Lobularia

Botanical Name: *Lobularia* hybrid
Aliases: alyssum, sweet alyssum, sweet Alison

**Height:** to 20 cm • **Spread:** to 50 cm

Sweet alyssum has long been a treasured annual with a light, sweet fragrance and flowers like tiny white jewels. Unfortunately its finicky nature and intolerance of heat limited its use so that it has been increasingly left on the curb as the container gardening craze races on. A new introduction from Proven Winners is 'Snow Princess,' which is being trumpeted as the release of the season and could catapult lobularia back into the limelight.

**The Basics:** Lobularia thrives most in the cool temperatures of spring. Keep the soil slightly moist. Like all high performance annuals, lobularia will need regular fertilizing.

**Recommended Varieties:** 'Snow Princess' is the new introduction. It is touted to be much more heat tolerant than traditional alyssum. 'Snow Princess' will bloom longer than classic lobularia because it is sterile and won't go to seed right after flowering.

**Best Uses:** As the 'Snow Princess' is brand new I haven't had a chance to trial it with anything, but it seems to have a pleasing enough shape to be planted on its own. For a mixed container, try pairing it with other vigorous cool-season annuals such as nemesia or diascia.

With all this talk about the new and improved variety, however, keep in mind that traditional lobularia is a wonderful annual if used properly. For a low cost, high reward spring container, it's delightful when paired with some simple violas and/or nemesia.

**Things to Know:** Lobularia tends to shed flowers, so try not to hang it over other plants or it could make a mess in the soil.

A gorgeous border of old-fashioned lobularia.

# Million Bells

**Botanical Name:** *Calibrachoa* hybrids
Aliases: calibrachoa

**Height:** to 35 cm • **Spread:** to 50 cm

These are my favourite container stuffers! They're closely related to petunias, and were in fact hybridized alongside them over 100 years ago, but the larger-flowered petunias were the favourite and million bells were forgotten until the 1990s. They're smaller but flower more prolifically, have a more appealing shape and lack that annoying petunia stickiness on their leaves. You know what I mean—it gets on your fingers and your clothes and just plain everywhere! Every garden should have some million bells in it. There are now dozens of colours, and they grow like crazy and bloom all summer with minimal deadheading. If you're a gardening rookie who wants to look like a pro, plant these flowers, then sit back and soak up the praise!

**The Basics:** Million bells perform best in full sun but can handle some light shade. They are more drought tolerant than petunias and prefer to dry slightly between waterings. Fertilize regularly to keep them firm and prolific. They are fuelled by the sun and bloom best and stay most compact when there's lots of it. If you have a long string of cloudy weather, they will bloom less and get leggy; it is best to pinch them back lightly, fertilize and wait.

**Recommended Varieties:** An important caveat before I recommend: any variety of calibrachoa is only as good as its grower. If you buy a recommended variety from a poor grower, you're going to end up with a

'Superbells Plum' is one of our most popular varieties thanks to its extra large flowers.

Million bells work well for landscape plantings.

Yellow million bells look great with lime sweet potato vine.

poor plant unless your thumb is extra green. Buy a no-name variety from a good grower, and you'll probably get a good plant. Look for plants that are well branched and firm (give them a gentle shake), and avoid them if they've been waterlogged.

Million bells, like bacopa or ketchup, is a brand name that has become so ubiquitous that it is often the accepted name. Calibrachoa is more proper but isn't nearly as catchy. My

recommended series is **Superbells**, which boasts the largest flowers (some almost as large as trailing petunias), has the best heat tolerance and is the hardest for us to keep on the shelves. There are new colours coming out every year, and while they often have slightly different habits from each other, they are virtuosos in the garden. **Callie** is a wonderful series with particularly vibrant colour if grown well, and it blooms very quickly. **Can-Can** is a

A basket of million bells often looks this good with minimal effort.

new series that features a new cream and brown **'Mocha'** colour.

**Best Uses:** Million bells are very versatile and can steal any show. When you're thinking about the flowers in mixed planters, think of them as both trailers and fillers; while they slightly cascade, they also take up a lot of room above the rim. They have such a terrific habit that I usually plant them on their own or just with some bacopa, creeping Jenny or sweet potato vine to accent. When I do put them in a mixed container, I like them with euphorbia, osteospermum, trailing verbena and coleus. They won't do as well planted in the ground.

**Things to Know:** Watch for aphids in late summer and early autumn, though they often don't strike million bells as fiercely as they do petunias. This plant can get waterlogged if kept too wet.

# Nemesia

**Botanical Name:** *Nemesia fruticans*

**Height:** to 40 cm • **Spread:** to 30 cm

Nemesia is a cool-season gem that explodes into clusters of delicate, often fragrant flowers in spring. It's easy to care for and is a perfect way to get the season started while other annuals are still growing and the perennials are just waking up. Recent introductions have given nemesia more colour, scent and heat tolerance than ever before.

**The Basics:** Nemesia loves the cool weather of a mild spring, and for this reason it will often be the prettiest plant in the garden centre in May. Plant it in a mostly sunny spot (protected a little from late afternoon sun if possible) and keep the soil evenly moist. It doesn't like a lot of humidity and will thrive most in the cool springs of drier Canadian regions.

'Sunsatia Mango' is a rich yellow/orange/purple tricolour.

**Recommended Varieties:** There has been a steady flow of new introductions in recent years, and different varieties have been bred for different uses. If you're interested in classic-looking nemesia, **'Compact Innocence'** produces a mat of delicate, white flowers that emit a lovely scent in the evening. **'Aromatica'** is also very fragrant. **'Bluebird'** boasts flowers that are a rare sky blue.

My favourite series is the **Sunsatia Series**. It is vigorous and comes in deliciously juicy colours, and with a little shelter and ample water I've seen it continue to bloom even after a July heat wave. Different colours of Sunsatias have different growth habits, so look at the plant before you buy it. For example, the red is a trailer while the peach is an upright filler plant. Sunsatia nemesias are not fragrant.

**Best Uses:** Nemesia is a perfect match with other delicate, cool-weather lovers such as pansy, schizanthus and ageratum. Try keeping some 'Compact Innocence,' with its gorgeous smell, in a small container on your patio where you sit, along with some heliotrope and lobularia.

Although the fragrant varieties tend to be delicate and are best in small containers, Sunsatias are more classic, high performance annuals that do best mixed with other container champions such as million bells, bidens and verbena. Nemesia also does very well planted in the ground, where the soil cools off the roots, and is an early spring favourite in rock gardens, where it will bring early colour while the perennials are still dormant.

**Things to Know:** Nemesia looks great in spring but may swelter once summer sets in. When this happens, try to give it some shelter and trim it back. With a little fertilizer it may send up a new flush once the weather cools off.

'Sunsatia Raspberry' is another of the fruit-themed varieties from Proven Winners.

# Petunia—Trailing

**Botanical Name:** *Petunia* x *hybrida*

**Height:** to 50 cm • **Spread:** to 1.5 m

Trailing petunias are the poster child of the container gardening revolution, and for good reason. In the mid-1990s Wave petunias helped pioneer the craze, and they still dominate containers all over the country. In drier regions like the Prairies, there are trailing petunias on every street corner. They bloom like crazy, are easy to maintain and are guaranteed to bring big, fast colour to your containers.

**The Basics:** The lowly petunia, plucked unceremoniously from the South African jungle in the early 19th century and brought back to Europe, has been at the spearhead of two giant leaps forward in annuals gardening. During the rapid suburbanization following World War II, breeders developed cultivar after cultivar, and petunias became a staple in front-yard flower beds all over North America. In 1995, Ball introduced the Wave petunia and yes, we were sceptical. Very few people believed the hype about 1 m in a season; those were simpler times in the gardening world when the only things that grew that quickly were beans and dill. Oh boy, have things changed!

This 'Vista Fuchsia' and 'Vista Bubblegum' mix has the most volume of any trailing petunias.

Petunias need as much sun as possible to perform at their best and can take really hot spots as long as they don't dry out. They need to be kept slightly moist, but make sure the soil is well drained or they will become waterlogged. Deadheading helps, even if they are touted as being "self-cleaning," and if they get leggy (which they will if there's a cool, cloudy spell), give them a gentle cut back. They need weekly fertilizer.

## Recommended Varieties:

There are several groups of Waves that you should know about when you're looking at that pink pot. The original **Wave Series** is the shortest, growing a maximum of 15 cm tall but spreading the most. **'Shock Wave'** has more volume, topping out at 25 cm tall, but doesn't spread as far as original Waves. **'Easy Wave'** is taller still, and **'Tidal Wave'** is the largest of them all, a shrub-sized ball of sticky colour that grows to 50 cm tall and spreads over 1 m. Of these, the purple and the pinks are the most reliable; blue is popular, but its growth habit isn't as strong.

Nothing beats the **Supertunia Series** when it comes to overall performance, colour, selection and durability. Different varieties of Supertunias have different growth habits. The newer types, such as **'Bordeaux,'** tend to have dense habits that form a compact ball of colour before they spill over the basket. Many of the older varieties have a more open habit. The compact varieties will grow upright until gravity makes them slump over, making an empty

'Raspberry Blast' is a sassy bicolour with a superb growth habit that has rocketed to popularity since its 2008 introduction.

space in the middle as they begin to trail. From here on if you have one placed where you can see the top of the basket, you may want to pinch the top branches back so they fill in. There are dozens of colours available; my customers love the daylight-extending **'Silver,'** the sassy new **'Citrus,'** the bicoloured **'Raspberry Blast'** and the always popular **'Royal Velvet.'** The new **'Silverberry'** is also a big hit.

If you're looking for really big colour, ask for the **Vista Series** (but don't say I didn't warn you). The **Ramblin' Series** is another one that has really impressed me, with great colours

such as **'Burgundy Chrome.'** It has a great growth habit.

Breeding companies market trailing petunias relentlessly, whether it's the pink Wave pot at the box stores or Proven Winners Supertunia banners at the garden centre, and every company has its own series that it claims performs better. Marketing is just another way the industry has changed; expect to see even more of it as more series are unveiled. Here is a (partial) list of some of the brand names you might encounter (each series has between five and 20 different colours):

- Calitunia
- Cascadia
- Charming
- Fame
- Famous
- Happy
- Happy Mini
- Littletunia
- Petitunia
- Picnic
- Potunia
- Ramblin'
- Rhythm and Blues
- Sun Catcher
- Sun Spun
- Supertunia
- Surfinia
- Vista
- Wave
- Whispers

There is an astonishing array of trailing petunias, but always look past the promotional hype at the plant itself. Make sure it's well branched, has dark green leaves (pale leaves

Waves are perfect for mass plantings. These are Waves in window boxes along the roof of Salisbury.

indicate nutrient deficiency) and has a firm and robust habit (give it a gentle shake). Remember that the plant is what matters when the fancy pot comes off.

**Best Uses:** The most common question I get about petunias is, "What is the difference between a Wave and a Supertunia?" It's a good question because they aren't the same thing. A Wave behaves like an ocean wave and spreads horizontally. Some of the best uses I've seen of Waves have been flowing out of tipped-over whiskey barrels. Wave petunias are performing workhorses, and if you want to cover a lot of ground with colour, Waves are the way to do it. I recommend them for ground covers, mass plantings or in borders.

For mixed planters and hanging baskets, I recommend Supertunias. They have a pleasing enough habit to be planted on their own and are more natural trailers than Waves, even though they tend to take up more volume. If you plant them in a mixed basket, make sure their container-mates are fellow "sharks." Try mixing them with verbena, bacopa, bidens, purple fountain grass or phlox.

**Things to Know:** When watering, try to use a shower-wand on your hose; a blast from a naked hose will hurt the foliage. Around the end of August—early September if you're lucky—your petunias will probably catch a bad case of aphids. Once they have spread across the plant, give up the fight; aphids have more reinforcements than you have patience.

# Phlox

**Botanical Name:** *Phlox drummondii*
Aliases: Drummond phlox

**Height:** to 45 cm · **Spread:** to 45 cm

Phlox has been a popular and versatile perennial and cut flower for a long time. Now, new varieties are making it sought after as a container garden annual; its broad, bright flower clusters and its long blooming season make this one well worth planting.

**The Basics:** There are many species of phlox. Annual phlox, often *P. drummondii*, thrives in hot, humid summers in full sun to partial shade, but it tolerates both cool and warm summers. Phlox needs to dry out slightly between waterings, but not not too much or it may stop blooming and go to seed.

**Recommended Varieties:** The **Intensia Series** is a low maintenance beauty that never seems to stop blooming! **'Cabernet'** and **'Neon Pink'** are the most reliable, while the bicoloured **'Star Brite'** has a less uniform habit but makes up for it with its unique striped flowers. The **Astoria Series** is also excellent. One of my personal favourites is actually an old classic: **'21st Century'** phlox forms an ultra dwarf mound with punchy colours. It doesn't bloom for as long as the new phloxes, tending to go to seed in summer, but it is often available in packs, making it more affordable when you can find it. The new varieties, especially, have been bred to tolerate the hot summers of the southern U.S.

**Best Uses:** 'Cabernet,' with its rich wine colouring, blends well with oxalis and citrus-coloured pansies. Match 'Neon Pink' with diascia and 'Cherry Pink' million bells for a whole lot of pink! Phlox's tolerance of alkaline soil also makes it a good companion with baby's breath.

**Things to Know:** Phlox attracts butterflies and other beneficial pollinators, but if you have a lot of rabbits

This 'Intensia Lavender' looks great with trailing petunias.

in your garden, they may turn your phlox into a stump. Also watch for powdery mildew, and apply sulphur dust if necessary.

'Lavender' is a slightly softer colour.

# Scaevola

**Botanical Name:** *Scaevola aemula*
**Aliases:** fan flower

**Height:** to 20 cm • **Spread:** to 1 m

Scaevola is an Australian native that thrives in the hot summer sun. It gets its other name, fan flower, because its flowers look like tiny Japanese fans unfurled by the dozens along arching stems. It won't really take off until around the middle of June, but once it does it's sure to impress. Scaevola is perfect for gardeners interested in the easy, eye-catching and uniquely gorgeous.

**The Basics:** Scaevola loves heat and tolerates drought. It requires very little maintenance and doesn't need deadheading. Even when the thermometer crosses 35° C, this tough plant will keep blooming and thrilling. Make sure the soil is very well drained; scaevola will tolerate sandy soil.

**Recommended Varieties:** **'Blue Wonder'** was one of the first varieties and still performs very well, boasting stems that trail up to 1 m long. **'New Wonder'** is also a reliable blue-purple, but there are other great varieties and colours available. The new **'Blue Print'** is the most mounding and compact variety and is ideal for smaller containers. Although blue and white are the most common colours, watch for blue bicolours and pinks as well.

**Best Uses:** Scaevola is very versatile and will do well with almost anything as long as it's in the sun, though it tends to perform better in containers rather than the ground because of the temperature difference in the soil. It is a uniquely shaped trailer. The stems arch gracefully upward as they cascade, making the fans look as if they're hovering on a steady breeze. I recommend scaevola with big volume annuals such as sweet potato vine, million bells and purple fountain grass. Its distinct habit also makes it a great creeper. Plant it in a shallow container above a rock garden or wall in full sun, and its stems will criss-cross around the stones. Or, with all the

'New Wonder' is a great variety for long, arching stems.

recent Australian introductions, why not try an Aussie container with scaevola, flambe and strawflower?

**Things to Know:** Scaevola doesn't like phosphates, so avoid fertilizers with a high middle number. Pinch off old stems before the wrinkled berries form to keep it blooming.

White scaevola looks great mixed with bacopa and white snapdragons in this window box.

# Torenia

Botanical Name: *Torenia fournieri*
Aliases: wishbone flower, bluewings

**Height:** to 20 cm • **Spread:** to 50 cm

This Vietnamese native is one of the jesters of container gardening, bursting with multi-coloured flowers that look like wildly painted trumpets bellowing out over the leaves. It's a heat lover that is easy to care for and is guaranteed never to be boring!

'Summer Wave' has the best performance of any torenia.

**The Basics:** Torenia is used to the moist, hot, dappled jungle floors of Southeast Asia. Allow the surface to dry out slightly between waterings and give it as much heat as possible without being exposed to the burning afternoon sun. I recommend morning sun or dappled sun all day. Plant it in a medium with lots of peat moss and fertilize it liberally. It loves humidity and will perform best in hot, humid regions. In drier regions the ideal spot is by a water feature. The higher the humidity, the more afternoon sun it can tolerate.

**Recommended Varieties:** There are upright and trailing types of torenia. For uprights, I recommend the **Duchess Series** (15–20 cm tall), which boasts mounds of colour in shady spots. **'Clown'** has even more vibrant colours and can handle more sun. For trailing varieties, **'Summer Wave'** was the first and still performs the most reliably. **'Catalina'** is a trailer that mounds before it trails.

**Best Uses:** Upright torenia sparkles in a small container. Pairing it with other jesters such as pansies and juncus will help to bring out its whimsical best. Trailing torenia looks beautiful planted on its own, thanks to its tight, compact habit. When planting torenia in mixed containers, remember that it performs best when it's hot but cannot handle full sun. Try it with other tropical annuals such as sweet potato vine, New Guinea impatiens or iresine.

**Things to Know:** Hummingbirds and butterflies like torenia for the flowers' nectar-filled throats, and some deadheading will help it to bloom more and bloom longer. You can bring torenia inside in autumn for a houseplant. The upright varieties especially should keep blooming on and off all winter.

'Clown' adds a saucy twist to this partial sun container with heliotrope, cordyline and Swedish ivy.

# Verbena—Trailing

**Botanical Name:** *Verbena* x *hybrida*
Aliases: vervain

**Height:** to 30 cm • **Spread:** to 60 cm

*Verbena* is a large genus with a fascinating history of myth, folklore, religion and gardening. Trailing verbena, which is becoming very popular in containers, is just the latest chapter in our relationship with this plant, a relationship that began in ancient Egypt.

**The Basics:** To be at its best, verbena needs 8 to 10 hours of good sunlight daily. It doesn't like to be waterlogged, so dry it out between waterings. If you also give it a decent amount of fertilizer and deadhead the old flowers, it will bloom like crazy all summer.

**Recommended Varieties:** The **Superbena Series** is the most popular series, with big, bushy plants that never stop blooming. I find that the **Lanai Series**, however, performs just as well and is available in a broader palette of colours, including the speckled **'Purple Mosaic'** and the deep **'Royal Purple.'**

**Best Uses:** Verbena is perfect for containers and hanging baskets that get a lot of sun. Its habit is different than most trailers, with stems arcing upward and growing more outward than down. This arcing shape makes it as much a full-bodied filler as a trailer, so I usually plant it in its own hanging basket, where it takes on both roles. In mixed containers it makes a great companion plant for other drought-resistant heat lovers such as gazania and million bells. One of our favourite mixes is to use verbena as a trailer with purple fountain grass or millet as the centrepiece, and 'Diamond Frost' euphorbia as the filler. You can also accentuate its unique habit by pairing it with 'Peter's Gold Carpet' bidens, 'Diamond Frost' euphorbia or 'Silver Drop' eucalyptus.

Pink verbena is vibrant and really stands out.

**Things to Know:** When verbena was first introduced, powdery mildew was a persistent problem, but since then its resistance is much improved. You will need to deadhead your verbena, but because it has such large flower clusters, it's not as much of a chore as it is with petunias. Like all heat lovers, it won't perform well if summer is cold and wet.

White verbena is a terrific accent with million bells in a sun-loving summer basket.

# Agrostis

**Botanical Name:** *Agrostis stolonifera*
**Aliases:** trailing bamboo

**Height:** to 15 cm • **Spread:** to 1.5 m

Agrostis grows like crazy, and while its bright green foliage tumbles down as tumultuously as a waterfall, it still manages to be one of the most graceful and meditative annuals available. It's a foolproof solution for a very simple hanger or container. My mother-in-law used to hang a basket in her old willow tree, where the cascading green falls would sway soothingly with every breeze.

**The Basics:** *A. stolonifera* is actually a type of creeping grass that is native to many parts of North America. I list it as an annual, but don't be fooled; I've seen it grow back after a zone 3 winter in a hanging basket. Soothing yes, but this plant is also aggressive and tough as nails.

Agrostis can handle full sun as long as it's well watered, but in drier climates it appreciates some shelter from the afternoon scorch. In hot summer it will need a lot of water, and it loves fertilizer; it will hang up to 1.5 m in the right conditions. Give it ample air circulation.

**Recommended Varieties:** There are several trade-names, but simply ask for agrostis or trailing bamboo. Not many garden centres like growing it because it's so hard to control, so it's often available only in large containers.

**Best Uses:** Agrostis' grace is as wicked as it is peaceful. This plant is stunning in a hanging basket or in a tall, upright container, but it is also one of the most aggressive annuals I've ever seen and will gobble up whatever it is next to. We've tried it with a number of other plants for mixed containers, including annuals such as trailing petunias and spider plant that are normally the bullies themselves, but they were all consumed! Now we plant agrostis by itself. It's perfect for oriental or tropical themes, and it will bring a trendy,

Agrostis is perfect for a modern look in a tall container.

contemporary look planted alone in a tall, narrow container.

**Things to Know:** Bamboo has a wicked reputation for naturalizing where it shouldn't be able to, so I recommend enjoying agrostis in a container where it doesn't touch the ground. You never know, and if it turns out to be hardy in your area, you certainly don't want it in your yard.

# Black-Eyed Susan Vine

Botanical Name: *Thunbergia alata*
Aliases: thunbergia vine, clockvine

**Height:** 25 cm–1.5 m • **Spread:** 25 cm–1.5 m

In 2009, Mediterranean colours (oranges, yellows and burnt reds) were the hottest trend going, and orange or yellow flowers flew off the benches before anything else. This vine produces scores of pure, warm circles of colour that are impossible not to admire. Thanks to its trendy colours and its foolproof, low maintenance, high performance style, it's one of the hottest vines around.

**The Basics:** Black-eyed Susan vine, native to eastern Africa, loves full sun, consistently moist soil and ample fertilizer. The traditional varieties are easy to start from seed, but the new varieties, which are the most vigorous, are patented and must be bought as starter plants from a garden centre.

**Recommended Varieties:** The **Sunny Series** is my favourite. They bloom early, bloom often and grow like crazy. The orange and yellow flowers are warm and vibrant. They should bloom all summer, and the pollinators love them. The classic **'Alata'** and **'Susie'** don't have quite the same vigour or colour, but they are still reliable, fast-growing vines and are lower-cost options that are often available as seed.

**Best Uses:** Black-eyed Susan vine is quite versatile. You can put it on a trellis in the middle of a large container (trim the lower portion if it's a mixed container) or try it on its own in a hanging basket. I prefer the latter because the vine will both trail down and climb up, creating a pear shape that obscures both the basket and the hanger behind a curtain of bright colour. You can also use it to climb a trellis against an unsightly wall.

Although it doesn't grow as fast as other vines such as cobaea, its foliage is cleaner and nicer to look at. All it needs to look great is a light trellis to climb. It grows by twining around supports for leverage, so building a trellis can be as easy as twining strong fishing line up a wall—you don't need to spend a lot of money. My wife makes teepees of bamboo poles and wraps mesh fencing or heavy fishing line around them.

**Things to Know:** It's an aggressive vine, so if you plant it in a mixed planter you'll need to protect the other plants by trimming back the black-eyed Susan vine.

'Sunny' is so versatile that it can be a trailer or a climber.

# Bougainvillea

**Botanical Name:** *Bougainvillea spectabilis*
**Aliases:** paper flower

---

**Height:** to 2 m • **Spread:** to 2 m

I often notice customers staring wistfully at the bougainvilleas on display at the greenhouse, and when I ask them why they usually share a memory with me of Sicily, Thailand, Hawaii or California that seeing those papery flowers again has made them remember. Bougainvilleas are beloved around the world for their versatility, colour and beauty.

**The Basics:** "Boogies" are easy to take care of as long as they are in the right spot. They love full sun and tolerate chilly nights better than mandevilla. I recommend boogies to gardeners on the Prairies because though they can tolerate humidity, they grow well without it. Let the soil visibly dry between waterings. Boogies have fragile root systems and can't handle wet feet. If you water them too often or (worse) leave yours in a saucer full of water outside, they will lose a lot of leaves, buds and flowers. When they are too dry, they will wilt but bounce back nicely—just don't make a habit out of waiting for them to wilt. Prune your boogies in early spring because they will need new growth to bloom in summer.

Orange or apricot is one of the harder colours to find but is worth it.

**Recommended Varieties:** Although popular in the southern U.S., bougainvillea has typically been expensive and/or hard to find in Canada, especially in the west, because of its tendency to defoliate after about two days in a truck trailer (a big problem considering it usually has to be shipped from fields in Florida). The bougainvillea that does appear on garden centre shelves tends to be the basic purples and pinks, which will give you the best performance. There are actually dozens of colours of bougainvillea, from reds to pink blush to variegated leaves, and if you can find an exotic colour, hold onto it and soon people will be asking you for cuttings.

**Best Uses:** Bougainvillea loves hot, sunny spots, so if you have a south-facing deck and a tall, narrow trellis, you will have a showstopper that will bloom all summer. If you think that your spot might be too hot, it's probably perfect. Bougainvillea doesn't grab onto and absorb other plants, so it is one of the best vines for mixed containers.

**Things to Know:** Bougainvillea isn't known for attracting anything especially nasty, but make sure to treat it several times with insecticidal soap before bringing it inside for winter. It has sharp spines that get larger (and pointier) as they mature, and like all pointy things, they can really hurt.

'Blush' is sometimes also called 'Appleblossom.'

# Cobaea

**Botanical Name:** *Cobaea scandens*
Aliases: cathedral bells, cup and saucer vine

**Height:** to 4 m • **Spread:** to 4 m

Native to Central and South America, cobaea has been popular for over a century because of its vigorous habit and large, unique flowers It is a late bloomer, typically not blooming until July, but once it does bloom the flowers are show-stoppers that go on to produce decorative seedpods.

**The Basics:** Cobaea is a popular and very aggressive vine that grows and climbs like crazy. It climbs by wrapping small but strong tendrils around anything it can find to pull itself up. If you hold your fingertip against the end of a tendril (on the tiny suction fingers) for a minute and pull away, it will even give a little jerk because it is actually suctioned to your finger!

It likes sun, heat and as much fertilizer as you want to give it. Cobaea won't bloom until mid to late summer, and yes, the flowers really do look like miniature dark blue cup and saucer sets.

**Recommended Varieties:** *C. scandens* is the classic type. 'Alba' is a slower-growing cultivar with white flowers.

**Best Uses:** Cobaea is the heavy artillery of annual vines. It's ideal when planted somewhere that it can grow rapidly and unimpeded. If you want to cover your fence with another buffer from the nosy neighbour, plant cobaea. I don't recommend planting it with anything else; its favourite pastime is gobbling up anything and everything next to it.

Its tendrils have sticky suckers on their tips for grabbing.

Cobaea is excellent for climbing around and over gazebos and arbours. At the greenhouse we have two planters at the front door with pillars in them, 4.5 m apart and 3.6 m tall and with a trellised roof. When we plant cobaea at each pillar, the plants will grow into each other by the end of July for a total of about 6 m of growth each!

**Things to Know:** The foliage tends to turn a shaggy yellow as August sets in. It usually gets aphids at the end of summer, and getting rid of them is typically a losing battle.

# Creeping Jenny

**Botanical Name:** *Lysimachia nummularia*
Aliases: golden moneywort

**Height:** to 10 cm • **Spread:** to 60 cm

Creeping Jenny has been around a long time as a low, low groundcover but lately has enjoyed a renaissance as a container plant. Its zesty colour and symmetrically alternating, chartreuse, round leaves have become a favourite in gardening magazines and featured containers. This plant definitely makes the "Hot" list for most trendy plant.

**The Basics:** Plant creeping Jenny in rich soil protected from the afternoon sun. It always wants to be kept moist. It will grow in full sun if given enough water, but its chartreuse leaves will tend to fade to pale yellow.

**Recommended Varieties:** **'Golden Aurea'** is the most popular variety, with chartreuse leaves that turn greener as they age. There is a green creeping Jenny as well.

**Best Uses:** Creeping Jenny is very versatile. It is spectacular in a hanging basket because its stems hang straight down, highlighting its symmetry. It's short, growing only about 4–5 cm tall, so it's a true trailer and will seem to spill out from the bottom of your mounding filler plants. Its straight symmetry also makes it compatible with many shade-loving foliage or architectural plants such as croton.

Creeping Jenny doesn't take up any space in the container; it's the perfect trailer.

Here it is mixed with trailing petunias and lilac verbena.

Although creeping Jenny has a reputation for bullying other plants, it is a great choice for a groundcover around a pond or water feature. It's also perfect for cascading down a rock or brick wall, though it will be happiest where it's always wet.

**Things to Know:** In some parts of the U.S. it's banned from sale because of its aggressive nature. In warmer areas of Canada I recommend erring on the safe side and keeping it confined to container gardens where it doesn't touch the ground to make sure it doesn't take root.

# Dichondra

Botanical Name: *Dichondra argentea*
Aliases: kidney weed, silver ponyfoot

**Height:** to 10 cm • **Spread:** to 1 m

Looking like long chains of silver coins that almost shimmer in the heat, dichondra is an ideal summer vine for modern containers. Its unique colour has brought it quick popularity from gardeners eager for something different. Native to Texas and Mexico, it was actually popular in California in the 1960s as a lawn substitute. Now, its gorgeous silver strands seem to be showing up everywhere!

**The Basics:** Dichondra is a heat-loving trailer that will trail 90 cm or more in the hot sun. It's very short and typically won't grow more than a few centimetres tall, so it won't compete for space with your filler plants. As it spreads, it can root from each leaf node and quickly form a groundcover.

**Recommended Varieties:** 'Silver Falls' is the most popular variety. It's a slow starter in the cool spring, but once the heat of June and July comes around it will be a real garden eye-grabber. There are green varieties available, but in my opinion the charm of dichondra is in the silver tones.

**Best Uses:** Even though it's officially a groundcover, dichondra performs best where it has room to hang freely. That being said, if you have a sunny space in the garden that you want to fill with a groundcover, dichondra is a good option because it will spread quickly. Try it in a container with other summer annuals such as grasses, pentas and million bells—just keep in mind that it won't really begin to perform until about late June. Its intriguing fuzzy foliage will soften the look of a container, and its silver hue will add subtle drama as it flows down. A raised bed or a hanging basket in late summer with dichondra flowing out of it is like a soft suit of armour. It hangs in long, straight lines, adding a touch of architectural appeal.

Dichondra will make a sharp contrast with dark sweet potato vine.

**Things to Know:** Although dichondra is not hardy in Canada, its ability to root into the ground wherever it goes can make it very frustrating for a gardener as it creeps across the flower beds, choking out other plants as it goes. I recommend confining it to a hanging basket or a tall, upright container where it won't reach the ground.

It's not called 'Silver Falls' for nothing!

# Mandevilla

**Botanical Name:** *Mandevilla* x *amoena*
**Aliases:** dipladenia, allamanda

**Height:** to 2 m • **Spread:** to 2 m

Mandevilla has been around for a long time as a favourite flowering vine in warm regions (southern U.S. and warmer), but it's only lately caught on with the Canadian container gardening crowd. Closely related to dipladenia, mandevilla is native to Central and South America (mostly Brazil) and is as tropical as a vine can get, with broad, glossy, pink flowers that can compete with anything else in the jungle for brightness.

**The Basics:** Mandevilla was once a rarity but has become popular thanks to its performance on Canadian decks and patios. It is a classic heat-loving vine and needs to be planted in a container where its roots can stay out of the cold ground. It will bloom constantly as long as it has good soil, some fertilizer and lots of heat. It's sensitive to over watering, so let it dry slightly between waterings and make sure it's never sitting in water; opt for a smaller pot so it stays a bit rootbound.

'Parasol Red' is a very pure colour.

Consistent temperatures (more than a couple of days) of 15° C or below may stunt its growth for a while. It will perform better in hot, humid regions of Canada where the summer sun is tempered by a lot of moisture in the air. In drier areas, it will enjoy an occasional blast from a hose on the hottest days to increase humidity.

It will stop blooming as soon as the early autumn nights set in. To bring it indoors, cut it back to about the size of its original trellis, treat it (see Things to Know) and put it in a sunny spot. It won't look like much during winter, but it should survive, and it can go outside around early June. Water it sparingly over winter.

### Recommended Varieties:

**'Alice du Pont'** is the original mandevilla and is a reliable patio plant with big, pink flowers; it's also the easiest to find. For flowering performance I recommend the smaller, newer **Parasol Series**. Its flowers aren't as impressive as the original, but you'll get more of them and its habit is more compact.

Here is 'Parasol Red' in a planter in Quebec City.

White mandevilla has glossy leaves and yellow centres.

Mandevilla's growth habit is always a bit wild looking, like this 'Parasol Pink,' but that's part of its charm.

**Best Uses:** Try Parasols in the centre of a medium or large container, perhaps pairing them with a harmonic purple fountain grass or a rigid cordyline. 'Alice du Pont' is a larger plant that is best used in large containers or for a trellis or archway on a hot deck.

You'll find that the most common size to get mandevilla in is a 3-gallon pot (25 cm wide). Don't re-pot it; it likes small pots, and the best thing to do is to pot-drop it into your container.

'Parasol Pink' is very vigorous and loves the heat.

The bold pink flowers of 'Alice du Pont' are the largest around.

**Things to Know:** Mandevilla can attract mealy bugs, which are unpleasant white critters that look like prehistoric trilobites. They are hard to get rid of, so I recommend trimming back the affected areas. Before you bring your plant inside for winter, make sure to treat it with a few good doses of insecticidal soap and/or a strong hose spray to knock the hitchhikers off. The sap can irritate sensitive skin, so wear gloves while pruning mandevilla. All its parts are mildly toxic.

# Passion Vine

**Botanical Name:** *Passiflora* spp.
**Aliases:** granadilla, apricot vine, maracuja

**Height:** to 4 m • **Spread:** to 4 m

The passion flower is the most spectacularly complex bloom that I've ever seen. In the last few years it has become ubiquitous, featured in everything from gardening magazines to billboard advertisements as marketing companies try to cash in on its beauty. Forget all the pictures; you have to see it in the flesh to appreciate it. Not only are the flowers remarkable, but it's also easy to grow and boasts attractive foliage.

Red passion vines don't perform as well, but the flowers are beautiful.

**The Basics:** Passion vine loves the heat and will need to be planted in full sun, preferably on a hot, south- or west-facing deck. Plant it in very well-drained soil (you can even add gravel or a bit of sand) and let it dry slightly between waterings once it's established. It is better planted in a container rather than the ground because it prefers warm, semi-dry roots. Regular fertilizer will keep its foliage deep green and healthy.

**Recommended Varieties:** *Passiflora* is a genus of 500 species of vines found almost worldwide but has only recently become popular in Canada. Although passion vine comes in a multitude of colours and textures, it's likely that you'll find only the blue readily available (or possibly a red or a white at a large garden centre). For a more exotic type, you'll need to special order it over the internet. The genus includes passion fruit, though that species isn't commonly sold.

**Best Uses:** Passion vine is a real conversation starter, whether in the centre of a large container or against a sunny wall. Wherever you plant it, it will need something to climb. Although it doesn't bloom as often as some other vines, it has attractive, dark green foliage punctuated with artistically curled tendrils. The tendrils reach and grasp quickly, so if you plant it with other annuals, keep the lower portion trimmed.

**Things to Know:** Passion vines have small root systems, so transplanting one into a large pot often leads to soggy, rotten roots; they prefer small pots. If you bring yours inside in autumn, first check for bugs and apply insecticidal soap as needed.

The botanical name *Passiflora* refers to the passion of Christ upon the cross. The legend is that an Augustinian friar stumbled upon the flower somewhere in the jungles of southern Mexico in the late 1500s. He had a spiritual epiphany when he saw the flower and sent word back to Spain that he had found proof of God's approval of the Spanish conquest of the New World.

White passion vines will be hard to find but are worth asking about.

# Sweet Pea

**Botanical Name:** *Lathyrus odoratus*

**Height:** to 2 m • **Spread:** to 2 m

Sweet peas are living proof that gardening trends come and go, but traditions are timeless. To me, sweet peas embody the fulfilling essence of gardening, and I'm delighted to see that new varieties are being bred for use in containers so that a new generation can fall in love with them.

**The Basics:** Plant sweet peas in a sunny spot that doesn't dry out too quickly but still drains well. They like cool, moist roots and need regular fertilizer for their stems to stay strong. If you're planting them in a container, avoid clay pots, which heat up, and it will help to soak the container when you water. Sweet peas perform well with cool nights. They will stop blooming if allowed to go to seed, so to keep them blooming, nip off spent flowers as soon as they begin to wilt, or better yet cut them off in their prime and bring them inside.

**Recommended Varieties:** There are hundreds of varieties of sweet peas, and like all scented flowers that are hybridized, some of the fancy colours have had the smell bred out of them. I recommend the classic **heirloom** varieties (the big, mixed pack of seeds) for the most vigour and the sweetest fragrance. As for newer varieties, **'Cupid'** is a very compact (15 cm tall with a spread of 45 cm) type bred for containers and hanging baskets. It smells divine, and its twining foliage is almost as pretty as its soft pink flowers.

**Best Uses:** Sweet peas are perfect to soften a fence or garage wall. They can also be the centrepiece of a very affordable container. They don't need a trellis to climb; a teepee of three bamboo poles with fishing line will do nicely. Drop a generous number of sweet pea seeds into moist soil and make sure they have ample light to germinate and grow. By mid-summer you'll have a stunning vertical centrepiece. 'Cupid' performs well either on its own or in a mixed container.

Sweet peas' scent makes them one of the best plants to bring inside. Don't buy roses in summer; cut a handful of sweet peas for the simplest, most rewarding bouquet possible.

**Things to Know:** Sweet peas will perform better from seed than from started plants. If planting seeds, treat the seeds with pea inoculant (available where you buy seeds—instructions will be on the package). Sweet peas take a lot of nutrients out of the soil, so I don't recommend growing them in the same spot for more than two years straight. Watch for slugs in wet years. There is increasing evidence that the seeds are mildly toxic.

They are my favourite summer cut flowers because they make the house smell wonderful.

# Sweet Potato Vine

**Botanical Name:** *Ipomoea batatas*
Aliases: tuberous morning glory

**Height**: to 25 cm • **Spread:** to 60 cm

Sweet potato vine is one of the hottest foliage plants available for good reason. It grows into a miniature jungle, exploding with lush leaves and striking colours with very little maintenance. Sweet potato vine is sometimes confused with regular potato vine (*Solanum laxum*) or morning glory (*Ipomoea indica*), and it doesn't produce edible sweet potato tubers to eat at Thanksgiving. Who would have predicted that a close cousin of the humble sweet potato would become such a superstar!

**The Basics:** Sweet potato vine doesn't like wet feet, so allow the surface to dry very slightly between waterings and plant it in well-drained soil. It loves the heat, but watch for fading or burning in full sun. During heat waves it will need more water. Fertilize regularly to keep it vigorous.

**Recommended Varieties:** Its massive popularity is leading to a steady flow of new cultivars, many of which are excellent performers. Look for healthy plants over brand names. Choose plants with rich colour and that are compact and well branched. If it's bushy with good colouring and is not visibly waterlogged, it will grow well. If it has faded colours, avoid it.

I love the **Sweet Caroline Series** because it has the richest colours. The Sweet Caroline bronze is the deepest I've ever seen, and the black is the most sublime midnight black. The new **Illusion Series** boasts deeply cut leaves that look a bit like hovering dragonflies with thin wings. It will be an interesting architectural twist, though I prefer the lushness of the very broad leaves.

**Best Uses:** Many people are surprised at how much space sweet potato vine takes up and how fast it grows. We fill 30-cm hanging baskets with mixed varieties of it, and they become massive, portable jungles taking up as much or more volume than most of our flowering baskets. I recommend it for larger containers, where it can really grow into its potential. In a small container it will

Sweet potato vine grows larger than most people think it will.

still perform well but won't grow as large. In any container, leave room for it to act as a filler as well as a trailer. It also works well planted in the ground as long as it's not water-logged and the soil isn't too cold.

As a big tropical annual, it looks great paired with other biggies such as 'Blazin' iresine, trailing petunias, million bells, 'Gartenmeister' fuchsia, New Guinea impatiens or 'Peter's Gold Carpet' bidens. It also looks great on its own.

**Things to Know:** One of the only complaints I've gotten is about how fast sweet potato vine tends to dry out in small containers. Watch for slugs if it's planted in the ground.

Black sweet potato vine is enrapturing.

# Tropical Vines

Botanical Name: see Recommended Varieties
Aliases: English Ivy: common ivy • Zebrina: wandering Jew,
   inch plant, tradescantia, spiderwort • Spider Plant:
   ribbon plant, airplane plant

**Height:** to 20 cm • **Spread:** to 70 cm

This entry is dedicated to three often neglected plants that have been around
forever as houseplants and are now beginning to venture out onto our patios
and into our gardens. At the greenhouse, these are our favourite tropical vines.
I love them because they can bring colour, texture and lushness to baskets in
a way that few plants can. Often overlooked as container plants, they are low
maintenance workhorses in the garden and are definitely worth a second look.

**The Basics:** The care needed for the three recommended vines is very similar. They are easy to keep and hard to kill. Plant them in consistently moist soil, and give them some shelter from the afternoon sun. For plants that are often overlooked they are surprisingly aggressive, so you'll need to keep an eye on them, clippers nearby, to occasionally rescue a container-mate from being gobbled up. All three of these vines are very easy to root; just float some cuttings in a glass of water for a while.

**Recommended Varieties:**
There are dozens of tropical vines and small plants commonly available in garden centres, and I encourage you to be adventurous and try some in your garden this spring. You really can't go wrong with any of these workhorses.

**English ivy** *(Hedera helix)* can be an annual or a perennial, depending on the region. Either way, it will bring reliable performance and some proper British manners to your containers. It will grow as long as you let it and won't compete with other trailers for volume. In warmer areas, unless you want it in your yard, don't let it touch the ground. There are dozens of varieties available, from variegated to textured to (my personal favourite) a jumbo type with huge leaves. All parts of English ivy are poisonous.

**Zebrina** *(Tradescantia zebrina)* is my favourite tradescantia because it's a hanging basket showstopper. It

Spider plant is a superb trailer.

creeps outward in full, thick stems of variegated rich purple with glossy leaves, and its habit is trailing as well as mounding. Give it as much sun as you can without burning it because its colour intensifies with the more light it has.

'Purple Heart' tradescantia is an upright plant with a rich purple colour.

You can train English ivy to do almost anything.

**Spider plant** (*Chlorophytum como-sum*) is fairly common; we've all seen one with its arching leaves and long, cascading runners, but we might not have pictured it in a container garden. It provides both cream-coloured foliage and a unique architectural flair—especially once it starts to send out runners.

**Best Uses:** English ivy is not as tropical looking as the other vines but is tremendously versatile. Match it with other classics that need some shade, such as pansies, nemesias or dahlias. Zebrina is perfect with New Guinea impatiens, begonias or dahlias. Spider plant is a great container-mate with other aggressive plants that prefer a little afternoon shade, but

The many cultivars of English ivy include this duckfoot.

Zebrina looks great here matched with lobelia and torenia.

you will need to keep an eye on it; I've watched it gobble up a trailing petunia. Spider plant is also one of the top plants for removing toxins from the air, so, along with areca palms and Boston ferns, it is great to have in the home.

**Things to Know:** Before you buy a tropical vine, check to see how full the pot is. They are grown from cuttings, and good growers will stuff multiple cuttings into a pot to ensure that the plant grows full and beautiful. If there is only one cutting in the pot, you're going to get one long vine unless you cut it back and branch it yourself (which takes up valuable growing time).

# Alocasia and Colocasia

**Botanical Name:** *Alocasia* spp., *Colocasia* spp.
**Aliases:** elephant ears, taro

---

**Height:** to 1.5 m or more • **Spread:** to 1 m

If annuals were fashion, big leaves would be Prada. Gardening magazines feature them regularly in glossy spreads of what's hot. Tropical is in, and these big-leaved beauties are as tropical as they come. Not many people know alocasia or colocasia by name but almost always recognize them in the greenhouse. If you love lushness, you'll love these leaves!

**The Basics:** These plants like heat, but watch for burning in full sun. In drier regions, alocasia will need some afternoon protection. Like most in the Arum family, the flowers are somewhere between insignificant and unpleasant; nip them off so the plant focuses on its leaves.

Although alocasia and colocasia look similar, they have different moisture requirements. Colocasia is a marginal plant and always needs to be moist (or even wet), while alocasia doesn't need quite as much moisture, so let the surface dry slightly between waterings.

These aren't cheap plants, but they can be kept year after year. You can harvest colocasia bulbs just like begonias (see Overwintering Bulbs, p. 48), and you can pot-drop alocasia so you can bring it inside in autumn—but you may think twice about bringing Persian palm in after seeing how large it has grown!

## Recommended Varieties:

There are many species of both genera available, and cultivars are being developed as they grow in popularity. The most popular alocasia is **'Polly'** (to 40 cm tall and 30 cm wide at the top), which has head-turning black, white-veined leaves that will arc over a small or medium container. **Persian palm** (to 1.5 m tall and 1 m wide) is an alocasia that may be a nasty weed in the tropics but is a much sought-after centrepiece plant in Canada, where it can't grow for more than one summer. It offers

'Polly' is the most popular and reliable alocasia.

large, lush, elephant-ear leaves that tend to hover horizontally, providing the perfect shelter for tropical fillers nestled under it.

'Black Magic' colocasia looks stunning with brocade geraniums on a patio at Earls.

Colocasia is dramatic in containers.

Persian palm's upright habit and fast growth make it ideal for making a statement on your patio.

My favourite colocasia is the charcoal leaved **'Black Magic'** (it may go by other names, as well), though **'Hilo Beauty'** is worth trying for its eye-catching splotched variegation. The common green colocasia, although not as sexy as the dark-leaved, gives the best performance. Colocasia can be finicky because of its moisture needs.

If want something just plain massive, call around for xanthosoma, which is the original elephant ears and can easily grow to more than 2.5 m tall in partial sun. It will be hard to find but worth it if you want to make a big, bellowing statement.

**Best Uses:** 'Polly' is so modern-looking that it may seem out of place with classic bedding plants such as pansies or snapdragons, so pair it with other architectural plants, such as succulents, cordyline or eucalyptus, and it will be the defining element in an impressive contemporary container. Mixing 'Polly' with white datura and black sweet potato vine will give you a stark, striking look.

Persian palm perfectly and instantly defines a large container as tropical. Match Persian palm in any large container with other tropical plants that prefer shade, such as New Guinea impatiens, hosta, ferns, hibiscus or croton. It grows quickly, so reserve it for containers 75 cm and above across, and because the leaves tend to hover horizontally, I recommend adding some tall curly willow branches for extra vertical appeal.

Colocasias love being close to water.

Colocasia works well with other moisture lovers such as bacopa, juncus or even petunia.

**Things to Know:** The sap of both genera is a skin irritant, so wear gloves if you have to trim your plants (they don't typically need to be cut back). Although colocasia root (taro root) is a staple food in some parts of the world, don't take a bite if you don't know precisely how to prepare it!

Watch for spider mites during a dry summer and spray with a high-pressure hose to clean them off. You'll need to do this in autumn if you bring alocasia inside.

# Angelonia

**Botanical Name:** *Angelonia angustifolia*
Aliases: summer snapdragon, angel flower

**Height:** 25–60 cm • **Spread:** to 20 cm

This native of Brazil is a relatively new introduction that is quickly becoming popular as a heat- and drought-tolerant alternative to snapdragons. Its flowers are surprisingly delicate, like dozens of tiny orchids crowded on a ladder, but it is a tough-as-nails summer workhorse. It's a perfect centrepiece for people who love flowers on everything!

**The Basics:** This plant has a lot going for it; you can plant it in full sun and not have to worry if the spot is too hot—angelonia can handle it. It also tolerates drought and often blooms all summer without a break; the hotter the heat wave, the more it blooms. It needs well-drained soil and should be allowed to dry slightly between waterings. Deadhead the flower spikes before the seedpods form to encourage fresh growth.

**Recommended Varieties:** There are several sizes and habits of angelonia, from 60 cm tall for centrepieces to smaller, clumping plants that are used for fillers and landscape plantings. Check the tag before buying. 'Serena' (to 25 cm tall) is a compact variety that branches like crazy and produces scores of tiny flowers. For taller varieties, I recommend the **Angelface Series**, which offers the gorgeous **'Dresden'** and **'Wedgwood'** bicolour blues on robust, well-branched plants.

**Best Uses:** Angelonia is usually used as a centrepiece but, again, check the tag to make sure it's going to be the right size. The taller types have a more open, airy habit (like gaura but not as much), and while they make great centrepieces, they will look a bit out of place in a large container. 'Serena' makes a great filler plant in larger containers, where it brings a hint of verticality. I've also seen it used as a unique mass planting alternative or to bring height to a hanging basket. All angelonias are excellent for vertical appeal in a window box or a container against a wall.

'Serena' is so compact that we use it in hanging baskets at the greenhouse.

The unique flower spikes make fairly long-lasting cut flowers, and cutting them has the bonus effect of encouraging new spikes to mature. Some people say they smell like grape pop.

**Things to Know:** Watch for aphids and, especially during wet summers, powdery mildew.

'Angelface Wedgwood Blue' with red New Guinea impatiens.

# Banana

Botanical Name: *Musa* spp.

**Height:** to 1.5 m • **Spread:** to 60 cm

Although you'll never be able to harvest the fruit out of your backyard, bananas are quickly becoming popular as a container plant. Fruiting bananas are raggedy, massive plants, but ornamentals are quite compact, rarely growing more than 1.5 m tall, and their broad leaves can really start a conversation on the patio.

**The Basics:** *Musa* is not a tree but a herb, the largest in the world, because it doesn't produce tough bark. Depending on the cultivar, ornamental bananas can grow 1.5 m tall, but they usually top out at 80 cm–1 m, forming a leafy umbrella over the fillers beneath. They love the sun, ample amounts of fertilizer and consistently moist, well-drained soil.

The older leaves naturally split as they mature; it's nothing to be concerned about. You can either remove the older leaves as they get ragged or keep them; I prefer to keep them until they turn brown, but if you have a lot of other plants under your banana, removing the lower leaves will create a palm tree look and allow you to do more with less space.

This banana adds lushness to a container on a restaurant patio.

## Recommended Varieties:
There are an increasing number of cultivars being developed for ornamental container plants, but no one of them has become much more popular than any other. **'Little Prince'** grows to 75 cm tall and is perfect for medium-sized containers. Many bananas have red highlights on the leaves, which bring even more visual appeal to a container, especially if you're working with bright reds or yellows.

## Best Uses:
Bananas look great in medium to large containers. Their central stalk with paddle-shaped leaves arcing out in a canopy is so appealing on its own that I often skip many of the filler plants and let them stand with only some short plants (ferns or zebrina) or some simple trailers (creeping Jenny or dichondra). They love sunlight, so match your banana with heat-loving smaller plants such as lantana, alternanthera or sweet potato vine. Throw in some pentas for some bold red to draw attention to the red highlights on the banana leaves. If you want a bolder centrepiece, match it with canna lily, alocasia and New Guinea impatiens for a tropical container that will stop traffic.

## Things to Know:
Bananas are susceptible to spider mites and aphids if dry. These plants won't do well if brought in for winter; it's best to buy them fresh every spring.

# Bromeliads

**Botanical Name: see Recommended Varieties**

**Height:** to 40 cm • **Spread:** to 25 cm

Native to rainforests across South and Central America, bromeliads are a large and fascinating family of epiphytic tree dwellers. They've long been used as houseplants and in office buildings and the like for interiorscaping, and now gardeners are increasingly using them to create stunning tropical containers. They are pricey, but their exotic colour will wow you for months!

**The Basics:** Bromeliads thrive in the deepest, darkest jungles, where they receive only minor dappled light, and they need to be protected from most direct sun. They need to be kept consistently moist and prefer being watered into their cup (the central depression the spike grows out of). They also like having their foliage occasionally splashed with water for humidity; a sheltered spot by running water is ideal. A dry bromeliad will curl the edges of its leaves. If you want to give it a treat, put it in the bathroom while you have a hot shower and let it dream of its jungle homeland!

**Recommended Varieties:**
Bromeliads are quite easy to find, but there are different genera in this massive family. *Guzmania* has the

'Silver Vase' is an old-fashioned *Aechmea* variety that is still sought after.

*Guzmania* spp. have outstanding colours!

*Guzmania* spp. are perfect centrepieces for mixed planters.

classic vibrant spike and is the easiest to find. On **Vreisea** the flower spike is flattened like a pancake but boldly coloured. **Aechmea** is the 'Silver Vase' orchid that used to be very common and has fallen out of favour. For containers I recommend *Guzmania*, usually simply referred to as bromeliad. It's recognizable by its prominent and vibrant central spike.

**Best Uses:** Many people are initially turned off bromeliads because they tend to be expensive, but if you find a fresh one (see Things to Know) it will stay gorgeous for the whole growing season. Wherever you put it, it's going to steal the show! Try it as the central feature in a lush container with sweet potato vine, New Guinea impatiens, alocasia or banana.

Most bromeliads are epiphytes and don't need soil, as seen by this bromeliad tree at Kew Gardens in London.

**Things to Know:** When choosing a bromeliad, make sure you're getting a fresh one. The bloom is terminal, which means when it's done the mother plant will die (you can re-bloom them, but it takes about three years and is not easy). However, if you select a fresh one in late May, it will be beautiful throughout most of summer. Look for one that does not have any white residue on the spike (this indicates age), and that is definitely without any "pups" (mini bromeliads) around the base of it; these appear when the mother plant is on its way out.

# Brugmansia and Datura

**Botanical Name:** *Brugmansia* spp., *Datura* spp.
Aliases: angel's trumpet, thorn-apple, jimsonweed, toloache

---

**Height:** 50 cm–1.5 m • **Spread:** 40 cm–1 m

Once appreciated only by a small group of collectors, datura and its larger cousin brugmansia have broken into the mainstream. They are paradoxical plants: stunningly gorgeous and intoxicatingly scented but at the same time deadly to humans. They are both beautiful and wicked; handle with care.

**The Basics:** Native to the upper slopes of the Andes, brugmansia is slightly drought tolerant, grows up to 1.5 m tall in a season and can handle cool nights. Its flowers are pendulous and usually exquisitely peach coloured. Prune it into strong horizontal branches, and it will bloom in dense flushes that emit an intoxicating smell in the evening.

Datura is a small shrub. It's not a prolific bloomer, but the erect flowers are impressive when they appear.

**Recommended Varieties:** For brugmansia, the common peach colour or the variegated (go for the common peach for the most flowers) are likely to be the only ones available in garden centres, though collectors can find a host of colours on the internet. As for datura, **angel's trumpet** is the classic radiant white, while the **Ballerina Series** (to 70 cm tall and 40 cm wide) is double flowering and offers a stunning purple.

**Best Uses:** Brugmansia makes a stunning centrepiece in very large container, where it will absolutely steal the show. You'll come to love a large brugmansia, especially when it is fragrant at night. If you bring it inside over winter, keep in mind that it will lose most of its leaves during winter and will take up a lot of space. Another idea is to take a few large cuttings in summer (they are easy to root) and keep them in small pots over winter.

Daturas make excellent centrepieces in medium to large containers. The

A brugmansia pot-dropped into the ground with snapdragons.

shimmering angel's trumpet white (the purest white I've ever seen on a plant) is a daylight extender and will almost glow after dusk.

**Things to Know:** All parts of datura and brugmansia are toxic and potentially fatal if ingested. I don't recommend these plants for families with small children. Pets are usually okay, but use caution. Wear gloves if you're handling them extensively, and don't touch your mouth or eyes. The seeds are the worst; cut off the pods as they appear and throw them away.

'Ballerina' datura is beautiful but poisonous.

# Canna Lily

Botanical Name: *Canna indica*
Aliases: Indian shot

**Height:** to 1.2 m • **Spread:** to 40 cm

These brash foliage plants are very popular right now, and you'll often see them showing off their big leaves in magazines and on websites. They are reliable show-stoppers and versatile enough to blend with almost anything. If you like your leaves big and your plants lush, don't miss out!

**The Basics:** Cannas love the heat but need to be kept moist. They are marginal plants that are often grown in water gardens. They thrive in warm, humid regions, and in drier regions they will still put on a show with their foliage but may or may not bloom. If you are growing cannas just for the foliage, cut off the flower spikes as soon as they appear to encourage the plant to produce lusher foliage instead of flowers. Cannas appreciate organic soil with elements such as manure and compost, and some wood mulch will help them retain moisture.

**Recommended Varieties:** There are dozens of varieties. I find that the fancier varieties, including the variegated types, have a little less vigour than the standard types—the most vigorous cannas are the originals. **'Richard Wallace'** is an heirloom variety with a sun yellow bloom. **'The President'** produces reliably gorgeous foliage with a red flower, while **'Red King Humbert'** has beautiful bronze-red foliage.

**Best Uses:** Cannas are spectacular whether or not they bloom. They can be used in flower beds or in medium to large containers. Excellent container-mates for canna lilies include annuals that like a lot of moisture, such as New Guinea impatiens, bacopa and colocasia.

In autumn, canna leaves make beautiful additions to indoor flower arrangements. If you want to overwinter the rhizome, however, make

Cannas are useful as a bold backdrop.

sure to leave at least six healthy leaves until the first frost so the plant can store nutrients.

**Things to Know:** Although cannas like to stay moist, the soil still needs to be freely draining and not waterlogged or stagnant. To see how to overwinter canna bulbs, see Overwintering Bulbs, p. 48.

Red cannas look striking with creeping Jenny in this modern container at Salisbury.

# Cleome

Botanical Name: *Cleome hassleriana*
Aliases: spider flower, spider legs, grandfather's whiskers

**Height:** 90 cm–1.2 m • **Spread:** to 30 cm

Easy to grow and long blooming, cleome is a foolproof annual with clusters of curving stamens that look like a huddle of pink daddy longlegs perched on its stem. Its delicate texture and strong vertical lines make it an ideal versatile centrepiece.

**The Basics:** Cleome is drought tolerant but will grow better with regular watering. It loves the heat, and you can plant it in the hottest spot in the garden in full sun. Give it biweekly or monthly fertilizer. Deadhead the flowers to encourage new buds to form.

**Recommended Varieties:** **'Sparkler'** (to 90 cm tall) is the shortest cleome available and the best for containers. It blooms a long time and, if deadheaded, will bloom repeatedly throughout the season. **'Queen'** is an older variety that grows up to 1.2 m tall and is best suited for garden backdrops.

**Best Uses:** Cleome is one of the best tall annuals available. In flower beds, put it against fences or garages to soften the overall feel of the yard. It brings instant vertical appeal to containers and blends well with other, less vertical centrepiece plants such as purple fountain grass and gaura. Cleome tends to either lose leaves or have unsightly leaves on its lower portion, so I recommend planting it with some beefy, high volume annuals such as strobilanthes or cobbity daisies for a screen.

A few summers ago I saw cleome planted en masse in a row of ceiling-mounted window boxes down the length of the main street of Tours, France. Too high to be seen in detail, they nevertheless created tiny pink clouds across the sky.

Here is 'Spirit' cleome blooming happily.

Cleome is great for attracting animals, especially bees and butterflies but also hummingbirds. It has a gentle scent that most people can smell only when they're close, and there's anecdotal evidence that its musty smell repels deer.

**Things to Know:** Although they bloom for a long time, they will often try to go to seed afterward, and people in the warmer areas of the country should nip off the pendulous seed-pods to avoid it self-seeding. The spines around the plant's stalk may be an irritant; wear a long-sleeved shirt and gloves when handling cleome extensively.

This cleome makes a fabulous mass planting.

# Cosmos—Chocolate

**Botanical Name:** *Cosmos atrosanguineus*

**Height:** to 70 cm • **Spread:** to 40 cm

Not many people know about chocolate cosmos, but it's a great catch if you can find it. It doesn't look like much at first, and unless you know what you're looking for you will probably walk right by it, distracted by the flashier spring bloomers. But if you plant it in good soil in a sunny spot and fertilize it, it will begin to leaf out, bud and treat you to prolific vanilla-chocolate scented flowers that are strongest in the heat of the day.

**The Basics:** This little-known Mexican gem will grow up to 70 cm tall and spread up to 40 cm. It's not very drought tolerant, so make sure that it doesn't dry out too much between waterings. It prefers well-drained, organic soil. It doesn't bloom until late spring, but once it starts it usually doesn't stop!

If you are unsure about being able to acquire it again the next spring, you can dig up the root and store it as per a begonia tuber (see Overwintering Bulbs, p. 48). If you want to propagate it, you need to do so via division because this species is sterile and doesn't produce seeds.

**Recommended Varieties:** The new **'Chocamocha'** claims to be the chocolatiest ever, but I just ask for chocolate cosmos. You may have to call a few larger garden centres to find it, but it's worth it. If your favourite garden centre doesn't have it, take a moment to tell them about it and recommend it for next year. The industry is moving very quickly, and garden centres need feedback from customers to help them keep up.

**Best Uses:** Plant chocolate cosmos in a medium to large container with other sun lovers and near a place where you often sit for summer visits with friends. Its sparse habit mingles well with large gaura for an airy look, or put it with compact annuals, such as osteospermum or dahlia, to spice up the shape of the container from compact and flat to two-tiered and intriguing. As for colour schemes, it's

Use chocolate cosmos to spice up the profiles of otherwise flat annuals, like these Symphony osteos.

a perfect centrepiece for a chocolate brown or gothic-themed container.

Once the long summer nights set in you'll notice the rich vanilla and hot chocolate smell. People will ask you about it and presto, suddenly you're the gardening pro who knows just what to plant and can tell people where to find the good stuff. Chocolate cosmos makes a great cut flower if you want to bring the scent indoors to enjoy.

**Things to Know:** In humid regions keep an eye out for powdery mildew. To avoid powdery mildew, try not to water chocolate cosmos in the evening and trim some lower leaves so that air can better circulate.

Chocolate cosmos has a sparse, dispersed habit.

# Gaura

Botanical Name: *Gaura lindheimeri*
Aliases: butterfly flower, Lindheimer's bee blossom, appleblossom grass

**Height:** to 70 cm • **Spread:** to 45 cm

Gaura is one of my favourites. It's sometimes called butterfly flower because
you could mistake the flowers for a cloud of soft pink butterflies hovering
over the container. Long popular as a perennial and native to the southern
U.S., long-blooming dwarf cultivars have recently been introduced and are a
container gardening hit. The large gauras add grace to containers or flower
beds while the compact types add a blast of colour.

**The Basics:** Despite its delicate look, gaura is a rugged, drought-tolerant heat lover that thrives in full sun. Gaura doesn't like wet feet, so make sure you use well-drained soil. If you want to use black dirt, mix in some perlite or vermiculite to provide drainage.

**Recommended Varieties:** There are different sizes of gaura. Varieties such as **'Karalee'** are very compact and typically don't grow more than 30 cm tall. They produce dense spikes of bright, hot pink flowers. The taller types, including **'Ballerina'** and **'Stratosphere,'** arc sparsely flowering spikes 60 cm above the container, where the flowers hover like butterflies on a baby's mobile.

**Best Uses:** Too often container gardening becomes a competition to pack as much dense colour as possible into a small space. The tall types of gaura show us the beauty of sparseness as their hovering butterfly flowers, sometimes seeming barely attached, bring a whiff of calm grace into our yards and lives. I like to match gaura with colours and textures that complement its rare delicacy, like diascia, phlox or lobelia. You could anchor the container with a bold vine such as a dark sweet potato vine.

The compact types make great centrepieces in smaller, colourful containers, or try them as fillers in larger containers. I've seen containers that use compact gaura as fillers around a large centrepiece gaura, and the

Its airy habit looks like a diorama of hovering butterflies.

result is fabulous. Small gauras work well planted in the ground, as well, and can bring a lot of visual appeal as long as the spot is well drained and sunny.

**Things to Know:** Remove the flower spikes after they bloom to keep the plant blooming. Bees and other pollinators adore gaura.

'Stratosphere' gaura looks great with pink geraniums and 'Red Shield' hibiscus at Salisbury.

# Hibiscus

**Botanical Name:** *Hibiscus* spp.
Aliases: Chinese rose, rose mallow

**Height:** to 1.5 m • **Spread:** to 60 cm

One of the most recognizable flowers on the planet, the classic tropical hibiscus (*H. rosa-sinensis*) has long been a cherished houseplant and is now increasingly being found on shady patios and in large container gardens. Gardeners are also quickly discovering other varieties within the genus, and now hibiscus is being used for everything from contrasting foliage centrepieces to patio trees.

**The Basics:** Care varies across the varieties, but regular fertilizing will keep the colour of their foliage deep and healthy and all hibiscus need consistently moist soil. They love their leaves to be showered whenever possible; this simulated rain helps keep leaves lush and aphids at bay. Hibiscus will recover with water if they wilt but will probably drop some of their inner leaves.

If you have a grafted tree hibiscus, you can help it to re-bloom by watering it from a bucket of water kept on the deck. The water will be much warmer from the bucket than from the hose, and the tropical roots will appreciate it.

**Recommended Varieties:** 'Luna' (*H. moscheutos*) and **'Red Shield'** (*H. acetosella*) are the best garden performers. 'Luna' is hardy in some parts of Canada and boasts big flowers. 'Red Shield' (to 90 cm tall) barely looks like a hibiscus at all until it blooms. It is fast growing, and the oak-shaped leaves form a small shrub.

You can put the classic tropical hibiscus outside as long as you protect it from full sun. I recommend grafted standard trees which, though more expensive, come in a dazzling array of colours, from orange to burgundy to double-flowering varieties, and have a vigorous habit.

**Best Uses:** Lately 'Red Shield' has become a trendy favourite, often paired with a canna lily or purple fountain grass in the centre of a

Grafted hibiscus come in a staggering array of colours, like this star-shaped yellow.

whiskey barrel–sized container. It can be mixed with almost anything that loves the sun. Grafted hibiscus trees are perfect on sheltered patios, on their own or with annual ferns planted around their trunk. The ferns have the extra benefit of providing mulching protection.

**Things to Know:** Hibiscus are irresistible to aphids, which are easy to treat with ladybugs or soap. If you have brought your household hibiscus outside, give it a soapy bath before you bring it back in because it will almost definitely have stowaways that would like nothing better than to be indoors over winter.

Hibiscus trees, like this pink one I found in the back greenhouses, are great for the patio.

# Peppers

Botanical Name: *Capsicum* spp.

**Height:** to 60 cm • **Spread:** to 30 cm

The noble pepper needs no introduction. The vegetable has been around pretty much forever, and the ornamental pepper is a common sight at Christmas time. In the past few years, however, I've begun seeing these hot little plants in gardening magazines spicing up container gardens with their vivid fruit. Whether it's herbs, tomatoes or peppers, Canadian gardeners are taking a second look at the beauty of food in the garden, and container gardening with food is one of the hottest trends going.

**The Basics:** Peppers are native to hot, often tropical climates. They need hot sun and like to be planted in rich, well-drained soil. I like planting them in a peat moss based mix because it is very well drained, and the slightly acidic pH gives the peppers a sharper, spicier taste. They don't like to dry out and love a little cedar mulch if you have it. They don't need pruning or deadheading.

**Recommended Varieties:**
Ornamental varieties: '**Black Pearl**' is one of the few peppers with rich, dark foliage that darkens with more heat and contrasts well as a foliage plant even with no fruit. It produces round, shiny fruit. '**Calico**' is a new variety with white and green variegated leaves with a hint of purple. My favourite, '**Medusa**,' produces dozens of wickedly curved fruits bursting from its leaves like fire.

Edible varieties: the habit of **bell** peppers is tall and narrow, and their fruit can be green, yellow, orange, red or even chocolate brown. The spicier peppers are shorter. **Habanero** peppers are very hot and grow on a very compact plant. **Cayenne** and **chili** peppers are a bit more prominent, and their fruit is uniquely curved and textured.

**Best Uses:** All peppers are excellent for containers. I don't recommend planting peppers in the ground because it stays cold long after the last frosts of spring, potentially stunting the peppers' growth. They look fabulous in mixed containers with other tropical heat lovers such as pentas, alternanthera and canna lilies. You may want to mix peppers with container-mates with a lot of colour so that there is more than just green when the peppers don't have any fruit. I recommend ornamental types as a centrepiece for small containers or as a unique filler for larger pots.

**Things to Know:** Spider mites love peppers, but you can get rid of them by rinsing the foliage down with a hose. Wash the edible peppers before eating, especially if you plant them with non-edible plants. Although many people eat ornamental peppers, I don't recommend it as some aren't at all edible.

These chili peppers look great in this Thai recipe planter with basil and lemon grass.

# Sunflower

**Botanical Name:** *Helianthus annuus*

**Height:** 35 cm–1.8 m • **Spread:** 20–40 cm

At the beginning of the 16th century, Francisco Pizarro, having found the Incas worshipping their sun god with sunflowers, stole several large sunflowers made of solid gold and sent them back to Europe. Today, it's impossible not to love their bold, bright beauty. Their simple charm never goes out of style, and now gardeners can choose from many sizes and even colours of sunflowers for their yards and containers.

**The Basics:** Plant sunflowers in full sun. Sunflowers that receive a lot of sun grow strong stems and large flowers and bloom more often than sunflowers in partial shade or dappled light. They like well-drained soil but don't like to dry out; use some organic mulch to help retain moisture. The giant sunflowers don't like to be transplanted, so direct seed them into the ground in spring.

'Teddy Bear' is an adorable double sunflower good for containers.

**Recommended Varieties:** The giant sunflowers are easily started from seed. If you're interested in a smaller variety, I recommend **'Ballad'** (to 70 cm tall). It has a long blooming time, often boasting multiple blooms at once, and it is compact enough to blend well with container-mates. It's also hypo-allergenic, meaning that it doesn't throw pollen around the yard, so it's okay for people with allergies. **'Teddy Bear'** (to 40 cm tall) is an adorable double-flowering sunflower that adds a unique touch to a garden.

**Best Uses:** Sunflowers, especially the big 1.8 m tall plants, attract lots of wildlife. Butterflies and bees love the tiny florets. When the heads are heavy with seeds, birds love to perch and pry them out, slowly hollowing out the head. Some people even cut off the seed heads and put them directly onto the bird feeder, but beware that squirrels will steal all the seeds from a planter but have trouble reaching them on the plant.

For container gardening, try mixing dwarf sunflowers with 'Purple Baron' millet, bidens and/or black sweet potato vine, or just put a pot of them on the patio table with some violas planted around the base and enjoy their ageless charm.

**Things to Know:** Watch for powdery mildew if your sunflowers are close together with other plants.

Sunflowers can make an impressive mass planting.

# Trachelium

Botanical Name: *Trachelium caeruleum*
Aliases: blue throatwort, blue lace flower, umbrella flower,
  purple umbrella

**Height:** to 60 cm • **Spread:** to 40 cm

In its native Mediterranean, trachelium is usually known by the unappealing name of throatwort. Canadian gardeners, attracted to its clusters of tubular flowers and its rich colour, have recently begun using it in their gardens. For a low maintenance centrepiece that blooms for a long time and is a magnet for pollinators, trachelium is worth a try.

**The Basics:** Trachelium is undemanding and easy to grow. It needs a sunny spot in well-drained soil and likes occasional fertilizer. It is moderately drought tolerant.

Although it doesn't bloom until mid-summer, it certainly gets noticed when it does. Many people say that the flowers have a delicate fragrance, but just between you and me, I can't smell it. Deadheading the spent flower clusters will help to keep it in bloom.

**Recommended Varieties:** The **Devotion Series** is the most popular. Look for well-branched plants, and keep in mind that stretched or drooping plants will probably require staking. The blue and purple perform better than the white.

**Best Uses:** Trachelium is perfect in the centre of a large container or as a colourful backdrop against a fence or a garage. Although the top of the plant is stunning, the bottom half can get raggedy; it's a good idea to surround it with lower plants. It also has a classic look to it, and I would be inclined to match it with purple fountain grass, dahlias and good ol' pansies. Pollinators, from butterflies to hummingbirds, adore trachelium, and it will look great in an animal friendly garden with mixed wildflowers.

Its long stem and big colour make it an excellent cut flower. Cut close to the base when the flower is approaching its best (hard to do, I know), and it will last a long time.

'Devotion Blue' blends perfectly with this black sweet potato vine.

**Things to Know:** If you have sensitive skin, wear gloves when you're handling trachelium because it can cause irritation.

Use it as a centrepiece or on its own in a container, like this one at the greenhouse.

# Cordyline

**Botanical Name:** *Cordyline australis*
Aliases: Bauer's dracaena, red dracaena, cabbage palm

**Height:** to 90 cm • **Spread:** to 50 cm

For decades, the reliable dracaena spike was the only affordable and readily available option for a vertical statement in the centre of containers or flower beds. It was everywhere, usually surrounded by red geraniums. In the past decade many gardeners have been in open revolt against dracaenas, looking for anything but for their centrepieces. Cordyline's rich wine red colour and crisp symmetrical lines make it an ideal alternative.

**The Basics:** *C. australis* is a New Zealand native that, like dracaena, loves a lot of sun and heat but will tolerate partial shade; its colour will be richer the more sun it has. Don't let it dry out too much between waterings.

It's a fairly slow grower, so I always recommend a pot-drop with this one so you can easily bring it inside in autumn. It takes up very little room through winter in a well-lit spot, and in a few years will grow into an impressive specimen plant.

## Recommended Varieties:

Some varieties of cordyline are more architecturally appealing than others. Although they will typically be sold simply as "cordyline" or "red dracaena," check the tag. The best and largest variety I've found is **'Red Sensation.'** Its leaves have a more purple tinge, but they are broad and stiff, giving it a rigid, eye-catching architecture. **'Red Star'** has thinner, longer leaves and redder colour but is not as upright.

**Best Uses:** Cordyline is a versatile centrepiece. You can use it in traditional containers as you would a dracaena spike, with almost any other plants. Its wine colour looks beautiful either with harmonious colours such as 'Red Shield' hibiscus or strobilanthes, or with contrasting colours such as lime sweet potato vine or talinum. Thanks to its symmetrical appeal, it's also good for more contemporary containers with architectural heat lovers such as succulents and euphorbia.

Cordyline can be kept year after year and will become an impressive specimen.

**Things to Know:** In drier climates, spider mites can be a problem; spray the webbing off with a jet of water. In more humid climates, you might get slugs if you don't clean the brown leaves off the bottom as they die. Make sure to check carefully for bugs before bringing it inside for winter.

We found these cordylines at the Royal Alberta Museum.

# Juncus

**Botanical Name:** *Juncus effusus*
Aliases: corkscrew rush, common rush

**Height:** to 40 cm • **Spread:** 40 cm or more

Juncus is the jester of container gardens. Wherever you put it, its whimsical spirals transform the scene from a drama to a comedy. There are other juncus species that are as straight is this one is curled, but they don't bring the same attitude to the yard.

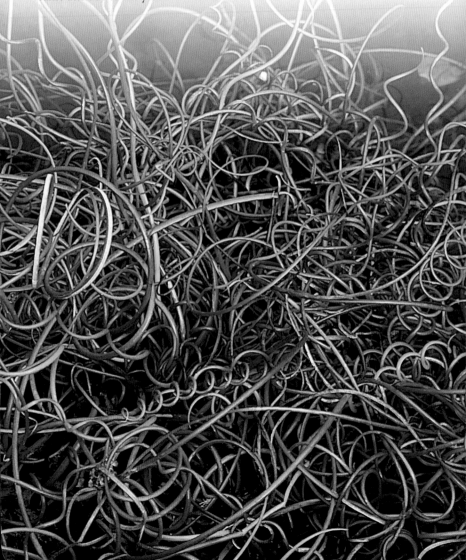

**The Basics:** Juncus is a marsh plant and as such needs consistently moist soil. Unlike grasses, its stems are thick and reed-like, and it doesn't grow very quickly. It doesn't mind acidic soil and would do well in a pot under a spruce tree. Try to protect it from the afternoon sun and fertilize it once a month, or it may turn yellow. It isn't a large plant and spreads as much or more than grows vertically, which will be no more than about 40 cm tall in a season. In midsummer you may notice unremarkable brown flowers.

Its habit is pretty much all over the place.

**Recommended Varieties:** The most common juncus has the characteristic spirals, and although it's sold until several brand names, the plant is basically the same. There are also several types of straight juncus, including **'Javelin.'** It boasts perfectly straight stems, which are very, very rare in plants.

**Best Uses:** This groovy little plant instantly transforms any container it's in into a whimsically modern design. Because of its high moisture needs, its uses are limited to other moisture-loving plants. Try it in a small container with some equally whimsical torenia and/or bacopa. You could also match it with a small peace lily (an easy to find tropical plant) if you're looking for a more tropical look. Juncus is a popular pond plant, but make sure to keep its crown above water.

**Things to Know:** It shouldn't dry out, but it also doesn't like sitting in stagnant water, so drainage holes are still necessary if it's in a container. It's tempting to touch, but try not to; its stems kink fairly easily and often won't un-kink.

Because it's a slow grower, some people pot-drop it and bring it in for winter to grow larger specimens. Make sure to keep it wet during winter, as well.

Juncus is perfect to spice up the broad, bright flowers of New Guinea impatiens.

Botanical Name: *Pennisetum glaucum*
Aliases: ornamental millet, black leaf millet, pearl millet

---

**Height:** to 1 m · **Spread:** to 40 cm

Millet's broad leaves, massive seed heads and rich colours combine to make a versatile centrepiece plant that looks fabulous no matter what kind of container it's in. It skyrocketed to popularity when it was released because it combines the grassy texture of purple fountain grass with the vertical burgundy of cordyline. It's also easy to grow but looks exotic enough to make you look like a pro!

**The Basics:** Ornamental millet is closely related to corn and as such loves the sun and boasts broad, lush leaves that have been hybridized into its characteristic rich purple colour, which becomes more pronounced with increased sun. It is not very drought tolerant and likes to be kept moist.

**Recommended Varieties:** **'Purple Majesty'** was the first cultivar available, and though it certainly turned some heads, its massive size (at over 1 m tall it can fill a whole whiskey barrel) limited its appeal. The more recent **'Purple Baron'** and **'Jester,'** both usually not quite 1 m tall, are excellent for medium to large containers. 'Jester' turns from playful chartreuse to red to purple-bronze as the season advances. 'Purple Baron' is my personal favourite, with its broad, dark leaves and stocky seed heads. **'Jade Princess'** is the most compact millet available. It grows to 75 cm tall and has full, broad leaves and beefy seed heads. It's also the first millet with lime green leaves, giving it a tropical feel. 'Jade Princess' likes warmer temperatures than her predecessors.

**Best Uses:** 'Purple Majesty' should be reserved for the largest containers or planted in a sunny border along a fence. Pair it with other giants, like 'Vista' petunia. 'Purple Baron' and 'Jester' are great for containers and contrast well with almost anything, whether it's for a classic, tropical or contemporary look. Try blending them with contrasting plants such as lantana, sweet potato vine or yellow black-eyed Susan. For an extra emphasis on the vertical aspect (if you have a very tall container and want to make it proportionate), cordyline goes nicely with millet. You can also mix millet with canna lilies for more vertical oomph. Just because it's a big centrepiece plant doesn't mean you can plant only one!

You can cut the seed heads for flower arrangements and crafts, but make sure to knock the seeds off the heads before bringing them inside. The seed heads have a delightfully tactile coarseness to them. If you don't use them for cuts, leave them so birds can pick the seeds out; the birds balance on the bobbing seedpods and peck precariously away.

**Things to Know:** In drier climates, I suggest spraying down the foliage occasionally to ward off spider mites. Although millet likes the heat, if it is in a hot spot that's also windy you may notice some browning of the leaves.

Millet is a perfect centrepiece.

# Phormium

Botanical Name: *Phormium tenax*
Aliases: New Zealand flax

**Height:** to 70 cm • **Spread:** to 40 cm

Also called New Zealand flax because the Maori used the long fibres for weaving clothing and baskets, phormium has become very trendy in the annuals world. Its long, sword-shaped leaves and vivid wine or pink colours make it a unique centrepiece. Although it's not actually a grass, it's usually sold as one.

**The Basics:** Phormium likes well-drained soil in full sun and will eventually grow into a thick, very impressive clump of vibrant blades. You can divide it after a couple of years, but I prefer one large plant to several small ones.

I would pot-drop this one so you can easily bring it in over winter. In a few years you'll have an impressive specimen, and it will usually send up a tall flower spike. In New Zealand phormium grows to be 1–2 m tall, though that height is very rare in Canada. As it gets older, its exquisite colour will fade somewhat.

**Recommended Varieties:** Phormium comes in many sizes and colours. The larger plants tend to be expensive, but you can grow a small plant into specimen size if you bring it indoors over winter. The colours range from green to hot pink, wine red, tri-coloured and near black.

**Best Uses:** Phormium brings a more defined architectural element to a container than many grasses do. The broad, rigid leaves provide an eye-catching contrast with many other annuals such as talinum, creeping Jenny and strobilanthes. You can also cut the leaves in autumn for cut arrangements, but I don't recommend this if you're planning to keep it over winter.

**Things to Know:** In drier climates, spider mites can be a problem; spray the webbing off with a jet of water. In more humid climates,

Red coleus brings out the colour highlights in this phormium.

you might get slugs if you don't clean the brown leaves off the bottom as they die.

This phormium makes an excellent fan-shaped backdrop.

Botanical Name: *Pennisetum setaceum*
Aliases: *Pennisetum rubrum*

---

**Height:** to 1 m • **Spread:** to 50 cm

This easy-to-care-for grass is the perfect solution to add volume, colour, texture and oomph to your garden. With its attractive arching habit it will take up some significant space in the container, but it's well worth it. It not only boasts richly coloured leaves and airy plumes, but it's also one of the only annuals that is gorgeous for all four seasons.

**The Basics:** This grass is slightly drought tolerant but prefers to stay evenly moist and will take a while to recover if it dries out too much. Its colours will be richer the more sun it has and will darken as the summer heats up. It doesn't like wet soil around its rootball, so don't plant it in too large a container or you'll stunt its growth.

**Recommended Varieties:** My favourite is the **common purple fountain grass** (to 1 m tall), but if you have a smaller container, try **'Bunny Tails'** or **'Red Riding Hood,'** which are compact, cute dwarf varieties that grow 45–75 cm tall.

**Best Uses:** A big fountain grass looks superb in the middle of a large container and contrasts well with pretty much anything. For a monochromatic treat, try it with Soprano Series osteospermum and black sweet potato vine. For very large containers, try some canna lilies in the centre with the purple fountain grass to accentuate the vertical aspects. For a sun-loving contrast, surround it with gazanias. Try smaller varieties with pansies and bacopa in a small container on the patio.

Fountain grass also loves being planted alone in a container that looks just slightly too small. It does best when it's a bit rootbound, and a fountain grass catching the wind in a tall, narrow container is magical. It does well in the ground, especially in a row against a fence.

I love the colours here with orange gazania and bronze sweet potato vine.

Purple fountain grass looks even better in autumn, and you can leave it while you either replace other annuals that have gotten tired or just take them out. In winter it's striking against the snow, and the seeds provide food for hungry birds, which will help to keep them in your yard for a natural pest control in summer.

**Things to Know:** Purple fountain grass doesn't travel well over long distances, so make sure the blades are healthy before you buy it if the garden centre doesn't grow it there.

This dwarf fountain grass is perfect with a bed of succulents.

# Sedge

Botanical Name: *Carex* spp.
Aliases: carex, leatherleaf sedge

**Height**: to 40 cm • **Spread**: to 20 cm

This is a quirky grass with a little attitude and a lot of texture. Sedge is popular for its coloured tufts of grass. Originally from New Zealand, it has been hybridized and used in gardens around the world, sought after for its milk chocolate colour and its brash texture. It is striking, coarse and reliable.

**The Basics:** Sedge is a sun lover that wants to be kept consistently moist. It is a slower grower than most other grasses, but it's worth trying for its rare brown colouring and tufted, slightly bristling appearance.

**Recommended Varieties:** The brown varieties of sedge are the most unique and popular. Different cultivars have different growth habits; some are pendulous and some are upright. You can tell the habit by looking at the plant. **Leatherleaf sedge** (*C. buchananii*) is one of my favourites. It arcs mostly vertically and cleverly curls at the tips, and its texture is coarser than most. You'll find brand names like **'Red Rooster,' 'Bronco'** and **'Bronzita,'** but look at the habit of the grass itself. Make sure you're getting a full tuft of grass and not just a few blades.

**Best Uses:** Sedge is not a tall grass like millet or purple fountain grass, so it's only a good centrepiece for a small container. Browns, coppers and bronzes are very much in vogue, and many people make a simple container with sedge and 'Tequila Sunrise' million bells. In larger containers, pair it with blooming sun lovers with contrasting textures such as gazania, lantana or dahlia around a taller central element such as gaura or hibiscus. It is a staple in any grass gardening—its colour and texture make it unique among annual grasses. You can also use it for a marginal plant in water gardening.

This sedge looks great in a rustic container with English ivy and Symphony osteospermum.

**Things to Know:** If the summer is cold and wet, watch for powdery mildew. Remedy mildew by making sure your sedge has lots of sun and air circulation or, as a last resort, sprinkle it with sulphur powder.

Small sedges in containers are like spiky tufts of brown hair.

# Stipa

Botanical Name: *Stipa tenuissima*
Aliases: nasella, Mexican feather grass, ponytails, Mexican
    needle grass, silky thread grass

**Height:** to 50 cm • **Spread:** to 40 cm

I always think of wood elves when I see stipa swaying in the wind, sunlight tickling its plumes. It's a delicate grass that's easy to care for and makes a perfect centrepiece for people who want a grass, but not the aggressive burgundy tones of purple fountain grass or the broad, brooding leaves of millet and cordyline. Stipa is a grass I can read a book beside, cover to cover, and listen to an afternoon swaying lazily by.

**The Basics:** Stipa is native to the southern U.S. and as such loves sun and tolerates drought. Its claim to fame is its eye-catching, delicate texture and its feathered seed heads that turn golden brown in late summer. Make sure its soil is well drained.

**Recommended Varieties:** There are several varieties of stipa, but my favourite is the graceful **'Feather Grass.'** You'll know it when you see it; look for the most graceful grass on the shelf.

**Best Uses:** I like to use stipa in smaller containers with a few pansies, dianthus and not much else. Keep this one close to you, especially if you have a favourite spot outside to read and relax, so you can enjoy its movement. Its drought tolerance makes it great for water-wise plantings, and its soft texture contrasts nicely with the coarse texture of rocks in an alpine garden.

I never take stipa out of pots in winter; like most other grasses, it still looks fabulous against the snow. If you don't want to leave it out for winter, bring it inside to use to complement a cut flower bouquet.

**Things to Know:** Stipa is low maintenance and generally pest and disease free. Avoid over watering, but that's about it.

Stipa has the most pleasing trailing habit of any grass.

Stipa looks great in a container with black-eyed Susan.

# Glossary

**Acid soil:** soil with a pH lower than 7.0

**Alkaline soil:** soil with a pH higher than 7.0

**Basal leaves:** leaves that form from the crown

**Basal rosette:** a ring or rings of leaves growing from the crown of a plant at or near ground level; flowering stems of such plants grow separately from the crown

**Crown:** the part of a plant where the shoots join the roots, at or just below soil level

**Cultivar:** a cultivated (bred) plant variety with one or more distinct differences from the parent species, e.g., in flower colour, leaf variegation or disease resistance

**Damping off:** fungal disease causing seedlings to rot at soil level and topple over

**Deadhead:** to remove spent flowers to maintain a neat appearance and encourage a longer blooming period

**Direct sow:** to plant seeds straight into the garden, in the location you want the plants to grow

**Disbud:** to remove some flower buds to improve the size or quality of the remaining ones

**Dormancy:** a period of plant inactivity, usually during winter or other unfavourable climatic conditions

**Double flower:** a flower with an unusually large number of petals, often caused by mutation of the stamens into petals

**Genus:** category of biological classification between the species and family levels; the first word in a scientific name indicates the genus, e.g., *Digitalis* in *Digitalis purpurea*

**Hardy:** capable of surviving unfavourable conditions, such as cold weather

**Humus:** decomposed or decomposing organic material in the soil

**Hybrid:** a plant resulting from natural or human-induced crossbreeding between varieties, species or genera; the hybrid expresses features of each parent plant

**Invasive:** able to spread aggressively from the planting site and outcompete other plants

**Marginal:** a plant that grows in shallow water or in consistently moist soil along the edges of ponds and rivers

**Neutral soil:** soil with a pH of 7.0

**Node:** the area on a stem from which a leaf or new shoot grows

**Offset:** a young plantlet that naturally sprouts around the base of the parent plant in some species

**pH:** a measure of acidity or alkalinity (the lower the pH, the higher the acidity); the pH of soil influences availability of nutrients for plants

**Rhizome:** a root-like, usually swollen stem that grows horizontally underground, and from which shoots and true roots emerge

**Rootball:** the root mass and surrounding soil of a container-grown plant or a plant dug out of the ground

**Rosette:** see Basal rosette

**Self-seeding:** reproducing by means of seeds without human assistance, so that new plants constantly replace those that die

**Semi-hardy:** a plant capable of surviving the climatic conditions of a given region if protected

**Semi-double flower:** a flower with petals that form two or three rings

**Single flower:** a flower with a single ring of typically four or five petals

**Species:** the original plant from which a cultivar is derived; the fundamental unit of biological classification, indicated by a two-part scientific name, e.g., *Digitalis purpurea* (*purpurea* is the specific epithet)

**Subspecies (subsp.):** a naturally occurring, regional form of a species, often isolated from other subspecies but still potentially interfertile with them

**Taproot:** a root system consisting of one main vertical root with smaller roots branching from it

**Tender:** incapable of surviving the climatic conditions of a given region; requires protection from frost or cold

**True:** describes the passing of desirable characteristics from the parent plant to seed-grown offspring; also called breeding true to type

**Tuber:** a swollen part of a rhizome or root, containing food stores for the plant

**Variegation:** describes foliage that has more than one colour, often patched or striped or bearing differently coloured leaf margins

**Variety (var.):** a naturally occurring variant of a species; below the level of subspecies in biological classification; also applied to forms produced in cultivation, which are properly called cultivars

# About the Author

Rob has been fascinated with plants since he was a child. As co-owner of Salisbury Greenhouse just outside of Edmonton, AB, he feels privileged to be able to share his passion with gardeners. He especially loves talking to gardeners who are just starting out and are eager to get their fingers dirty. His sense of inspiration is infectious, and he loves getting other people hooked on growing.

In his spare time, Rob writes poetry, climbs mountains in the Rockies, and works toward his Masters of Arts in Literature at the University of Alberta. He lives in Sherwood Park with his beloved wife Meg.